# Better Homes and Gardens®

# Cooking Mexican

Our seal assures you that every recipe in *Cooking Mexican*
has been tested in the Better Homes and Gardens® Test Kitchen.
This means that each recipe is practical and reliable,
and meets our high standards of taste appeal.

## BETTER HOMES AND GARDENS® BOOKS

Editor: Gerald M. Knox
Art Director: Ernest Shelton
Managing Editor: David A. Kirchner
Copy and Production Editors: James D. Blume, Marsha Jahns,
    Rosanne Weber Mattson, Mary Helen Schiltz

Food and Nutrition Editor: Nancy Byal
Department Head, Cook Books: Sharyl Heiken
Associate Department Heads: Sandra Granseth,
    Rosemary C. Hutchinson, Elizabeth Woolever
Senior Food Editors: Julia Malloy, Marcia Stanley,
    Joyce Trollope
Associate Food Editors: Linda Henry, Mary Major, Mary Jo Plutt,
    Maureen Powers, Martha Schiel, Linda Foley Woodrum
Recipe Development Editor: Marion Viall
Test Kitchen Director: Sharon Stilwell
Test Kitchen Photo Studio Director: Janet Pittman
Test Kitchen Home Economists: Lynn Blanchard, Jean Brekke,
    Kay Cargill, Marilyn Cornelius, Jennifer Darling,
    Maryellyn Krantz, Lynelle Munn, Dianna Nolin, Marge Steenson

Associate Art Directors: Linda Ford Vermie, Neoma Alt West,
    Randall Yontz
Assistant Art Directors: Lynda Haupert, Harijs Priekulis,
    Tom Wegner
Senior Graphic Designers: Jack Murphy, Stan Sams,
    Darla Whipple-Frain
Graphic Designers: Mike Burns, Sally Cooper, Blake Welch,
    Brian Wignall, Kimberly Zarley

Vice President, Editorial Director: Doris Eby
Executive Director, Editorial Services: Duane L. Gregg

President, Book Group: Fred Stines
Director of Publishing: Robert B. Nelson
Vice President, Retail Marketing: Jamie Martin
Vice President, Direct Marketing: Arthur Heydendael

## COOKING MEXICAN

Editor: Linda Henry
Copy and Production Editor: Mary Helen Schiltz
Graphic Designer: Brian Wignall
Electronic Text Processor: Donna Russell
Contributing Photographers: Mike Dieter, M. Jensen
    Photography, Inc.
Food Stylists: Janet Pittman, Maria Rolandelli
Contributing Illustrator: Thomas Rosborough

**On the cover:** *New Mexican Enchiladas*
(see recipe, page 20)

# Contents

**4 Tortilla Tempters**
Tacos, enchiladas, burritos, tostadas, and chimichangas—they're *all* here!

**24 Terrific Tamales**
Sweet and savory tamales—favorites from old Mexico.

**28 Chili Pepper Identification**
Learn which one's which, when to use them, and how to handle them.

**31 Appetizers Olé**
Fabulous finger food and fancy first-course fare.

**34 Sassy Salsas**
Snappy sauces for topping, dolloping, and dipping.

**38 Super Soups**
Potfuls of main-dish and side-dish soups.

**44 Mexican Mainliners**
Stick-to-the-ribs Mexican and Tex-Mex specialties.

**58 South-of-the-Border Sweets**
Mouth-watering sweet breads and desserts.

**72 Dynamite Drinks**
Flame-killing, thirst-quenching beverages.

**80 Tex-Mex Dinner**
A spunky Southwestern-style feast for 6 to 8.

**84 Mexican Brunch**
A midmorning meal with character.

**88 Fire Up a Fiesta**
A Mexican-inspired backyard barbecue.

**94 Index**

# It's All in the Roll

*Question:* When is an enchilada not an enchilada? *Answer:* When it's a taco or a tostada. How does this work, you ask? Well, all of the Mexican favorites that are pictured on these two pages begin with either a flour tortilla or a corn tortilla. Depending on how you roll and cook it, a tortilla that starts out

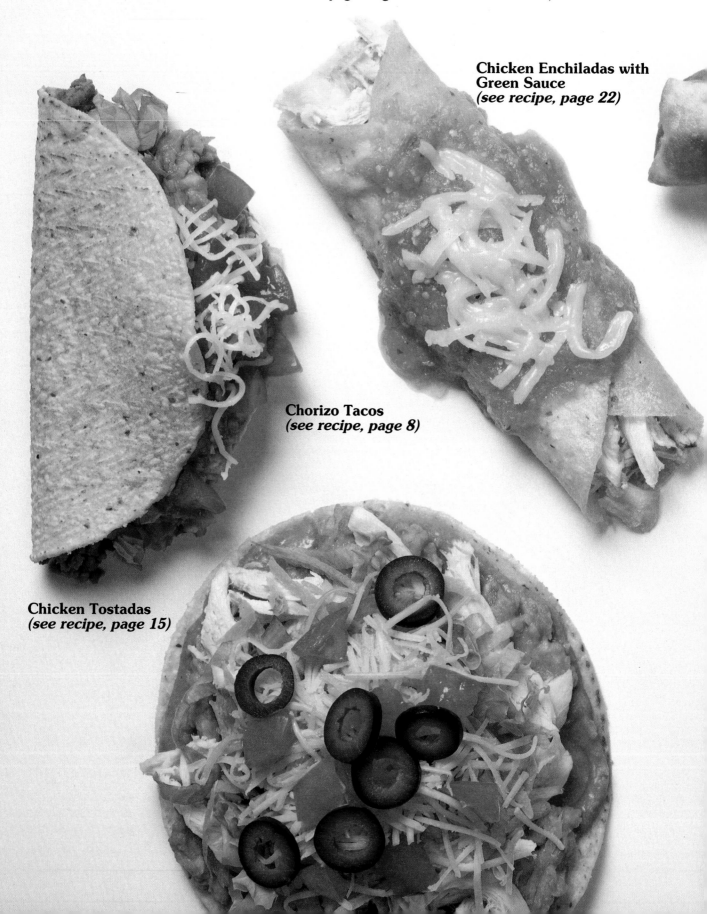

**Chicken Enchiladas with Green Sauce**
*(see recipe, page 22)*

**Chorizo Tacos**
*(see recipe, page 8)*

**Chicken Tostadas**
*(see recipe, page 15)*

as a burrito could very well end up as a flauta or a chimichanga.
NOTE: Traditionally, tostadas, tacos, flautas, and enchiladas are made from corn tortillas; chimichangas and burritos, from flour tortillas. But because we discovered that flour tortillas are easier to roll, we make our flautas from flour tortillas.

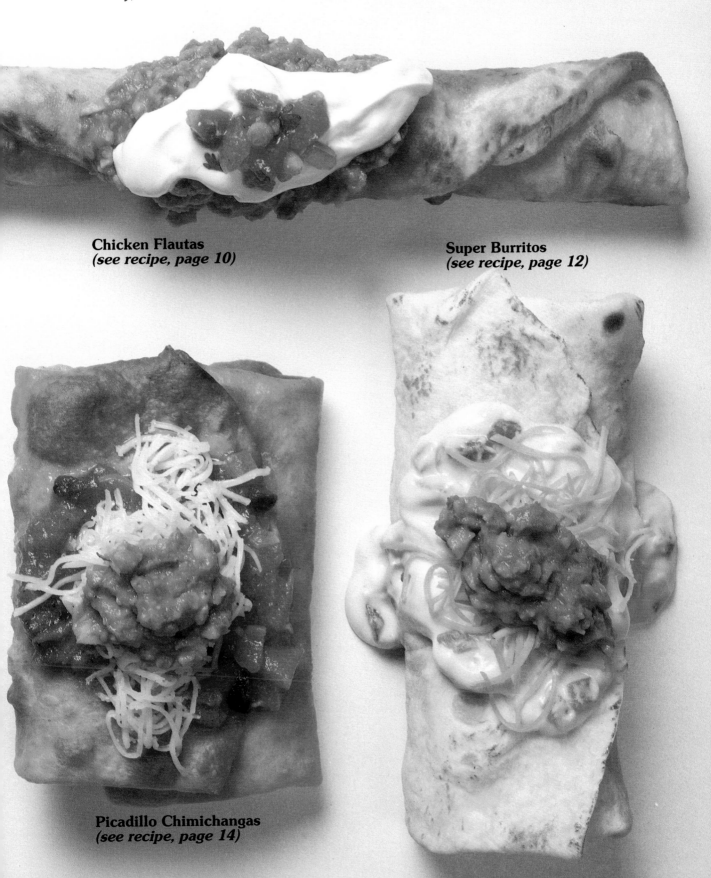

**Chicken Flautas**
*(see recipe, page 10)*

**Super Burritos**
*(see recipe, page 12)*

**Picadillo Chimichangas**
*(see recipe, page 14)*

# Corn Tortillas

2 cups Masa Harina
  tortilla flour
1¼ cups warm water

● In a medium mixing bowl combine tortilla flour and water. Stir mixture together with your hands till dough is firm but moist (if necessary, add more water, 1 tablespoon at a time). Let dough rest for 15 minutes.

Divide dough into 12 equal portions, then shape into balls.

● Using a tortilla press or rolling pin, flatten each ball between 2 pieces of waxed paper into a 6-inch circle.

● Carefully peel off top sheet of waxed paper. Place tortilla, paper side up, on a medium-hot ungreased skillet or griddle. As tortilla begins to heat, carefully peel off remaining sheet of waxed paper. Cook, turning occasionally, for 2 to 2½ minutes or till tortilla is dry and light brown (tortilla should still be soft). Wrap tortillas in foil if using immediately.*
Makes 12 (6-inch) tortillas.

*Note: To freeze tortillas, stack them up, alternating each tortilla with 2 layers of waxed paper. Wrap the stack in a moisture- and vaporproof bag, foil, or freezer wrap. Seal tightly and freeze. Thaw completely before using.

Plain, buttered, or wrapped around a filling, tortillas are found on Mexican tables at practically every meal. The first tortillas were made from corn kernels that were simmered in water till they softened, then were ground by hand. Today's cooks make corn tortillas from dried corn flour—*masa*. And *tortillerias* (tortilla factories) sell fresh hot tortillas throughout Mexico and in some large U.S. cities.

# Flour Tortillas

2 cups all-purpose flour
1 teaspoon salt
1 teaspoon baking powder
2 tablespoons shortening
  *or* lard
½ cup warm water

● In a medium mixing bowl combine flour, salt, and baking powder. Cut in shortening or lard till thoroughly combined. Gradually add water and toss together till dough can be gathered into a ball (if necessary, add more water, 1 tablespoon at a time). Knead dough 15 to 20 times. Let dough rest 15 minutes.

For 8-inch tortillas, divide dough into 12 equal portions and shape into balls. (For 10-inch tortillas, divide dough into 8 equal portions and shape into balls.)

● On a lightly floured surface, use a rolling pin to flatten each ball into an 8-inch (or 10-inch) circle. Stack rolled-out tortillas between pieces of waxed paper.*

● Carefully peel off top sheet of waxed paper. Place tortilla, paper side up, on a medium-hot ungreased skillet or griddle. As tortilla begins to heat, carefully peel off remaining sheet of waxed paper. Cook tortilla about 30 seconds or till puffy. Turn and cook about 30 seconds more or till edges curl up slightly. Wrap tortillas in foil if using immediately.* Makes 12 (8-inch) or 8 (10-inch) tortillas.
*Note: Freeze tortillas according to directions on opposite page.

**In Mexico and the American Southwest, homemade flour tortillas are more highly prized than your grandma's best biscuits! In fact, the art of making light, thin, and delicate flour tortillas is passed down from generation to generation. An old Indian saying sums up how Mexicans feel about their flour tortillas: ". . . children crave tortillas as a man craves good whiskey."**

# Chorizo Tacos

*Pictured on pages 4–5.*

| | |
|---|---|
| 8 6-inch Corn Tortillas (see recipe, page 6), purchased corn tortillas, *or* purchased taco shells<br>Cooking oil | ● For homemade tortillas, in a heavy saucepan heat 3 inches of oil to 375°. Place tortilla in taco mold. Fry for 30 to 35 seconds or till crisp. Remove from mold. Drain on paper towels.<br>For purchased tortillas, in a heavy skillet heat ½ inch of oil. Fry each tortilla in hot oil for 10 seconds or till limp. Use tongs to fold tortilla in half. Continue frying for 1¼ to 1½ minutes more or till crisp, turning once. Drain well on paper towels. Keep shells warm in a 300° oven while preparing meat mixture. (If using purchased taco shells, warm in a 300° oven for 8 to 10 minutes before filling.) |
| 1 pound Homemade Chorizo (see recipe, below), bulk chorizo, *or* bulk Italian sausage<br>Shredded lettuce<br>Guacamole (see recipe, page 16) *or* frozen avocado dip, thawed<br>¾ cup shredded Monterey Jack cheese (3 ounces)<br>1 large tomato, chopped | ● In a medium skillet cook meat till brown. Drain off fat.<br>Fill each taco shell with some of the meat, lettuce, Guacamole or avocado dip, cheese, and tomato. Serves 4. |

When it comes to making tacos, you have three choices. Try all three, then rely on the one that works best for you.
1. Make your own homemade corn tortillas from scratch (see recipe, page 6) to fry into shells.
2. Make "semi-homemade" shells by frying purchased corn tortillas (see photo, opposite).
3. Start with a package of purchased taco shells.

# Homemade Chorizo

| | |
|---|---|
| 1 3-pound boneless pork shoulder roast, well chilled | ● Trim fat from chilled roast. Chop enough fat to make 1 cup and set aside. Discard any remaining fat.<br>Cut meat into ½-inch cubes. Using a food processor or the coarse plate of a meat grinder, grind together pork and reserved pork fat. |
| ½ cup white vinegar<br>3 cloves garlic<br>2 tablespoons paprika<br>1 tablespoon chili powder<br>2½ teaspoons crushed red pepper<br>2 teaspoons ground red pepper<br>1 teaspoon sugar<br>½ teaspoon coriander seed<br>½ teaspoon dried oregano<br>¼ teaspoon ground cumin | ● In a blender container or food processor bowl combine vinegar, garlic, paprika, chili powder, crushed red pepper, ground red pepper, sugar, coriander seed, oregano, cumin, 3 tablespoons *water,* 2 teaspoons *salt,* and 1 teaspoon *black pepper.* Cover and blend or process till spices are ground. Pour spice mixture over ground pork mixture. Mix till thoroughly combined.<br>Cover and refrigerate meat up to 4 days or freeze up to 2 months. Makes about 3 pounds. |

Freeze hot-and-peppery Mexican sausage, chorizo (chor-EE-so), in ½-pound or 1-pound packages so it's easy to grab *just* what you need.

# Marinated Chicken Tacos

¼ **cup lemon juice**
2 **tablespoons honey**
2 **tablespoons water**
1 **clove garlic, minced**
¼ **teaspoon pepper**
2 **cups chopped cooked chicken**

● For marinade, in a small bowl stir together lemon juice, honey, water, garlic, and pepper. Pour over chicken, stirring to coat well.
  Cover and marinate at room temperature for 30 minutes or in the refrigerator for 2 hours, stirring occasionally. Drain well.

1 **cup alfalfa sprouts**
¼ **cup shredded carrot**

● In a small mixing bowl stir together alfalfa sprouts and carrot. Set aside.

8 **6-inch Corn Tortillas (see recipe, page 6), purchased corn tortillas, *or* purchased taco shells Cooking oil**

● For homemade tortillas, in a heavy saucepan heat 3 inches of oil to 375°. Place tortilla in taco mold. Fry for 30 to 35 seconds or till crisp. Remove from mold. Drain on paper towels.
  For purchased tortillas, in a heavy skillet heat ½ inch of oil. Fry each tortilla in hot oil for 10 seconds or till limp. Use tongs to fold tortilla in half. Continue frying for 1¼ to 1½ minutes more or till crisp, turning once. Drain on paper towels. (If using purchased taco shells, warm in a 300° oven for 8 to 10 minutes before filling.)

½ **cup crumbled blue cheese**
1 **large tomato, chopped**

● Fill each taco shell with some of the chicken, alfalfa-sprout-carrot mixture, cheese, and tomato. Makes 4 servings.

**Fry the purchased tortilla in hot oil till it's limp. Holding the tortilla with tongs, fold it in half and fry till crisp, turning once (hold slightly open to leave space for your fillings).**
  **To make taco shells from homemade tortillas, you'll need to use a special taco shell mold that holds the tortillas in shape while they're being fried (see photo, above).**

# Let's Have A Taco Fiesta!

Come party time, no food fits the bill better than *tacos*—especially if you plan a do-it-yourself taco bar.
  Arrange the taco fillings, toppers, and garnishes in pottery or wooden bowls. Buy packaged taco shells or shape your own (see photo, page 9), and serve them in baskets or gourds lined with brightly colored napkins.
  Take your pick from an endless assortment of taco ingredients:
**Fillings:** ground beef or pork, shredded roast beef or pork, sausage, chicken, ham, or chili.

**Toppers:** chopped olives, green peppers, radishes, tomatoes, avocados, hot peppers, or onions.
**Garnishes:** sour cream, guacamole, taco sauce or salsa, shredded lettuce, and shredded cheese.
  Refried beans (see recipe, page 87) are a must—serve them as fillings or as an extra side dish. Round out the menu with Mexican Rice (see recipe, page 46) and thirst-quenching Mexican beer. Finally, for an easy but satisfying finale, dish up ice cream and top it with coffee liqueur.

# Chicken Flautas

| | | |
|---|---|---|
| 2 whole medium chicken breasts (about 1½ pounds total)<br>1 cup water<br>1 cup shredded Monterey Jack *or* cheddar cheese (4 ounces)<br>1 4-ounce can diced green chili peppers, drained<br>½ teaspoon ground cumin | ● Place chicken breasts in a large saucepan. Add water and bring to boiling. Reduce heat and simmer, covered, for 20 to 25 minutes or till chicken is tender. Drain well. Let stand till chicken is cool enough to handle.<br>　　Skin and bone chicken breasts. Use a fork to pull chicken apart into long thin shreds (you should have about 2¼ cups). In a medium mixing bowl stir together shredded chicken, cheese, chili peppers, and cumin. Set mixture aside. | You'll play a new supper-time tune with these tightly rolled and fried tortillas that look a lot like the "little flutes" they're named after. |

**Overlap a couple of tortillas by about half (the two overlapped tortillas need to measure about 8 inches long). Spoon filling lengthwise down the center and roll up tortillas very tightly.**

| | |
|---|---|
| 16 8-inch Flour Tortillas (see recipe, page 7) *or* purchased flour tortillas | ● Stack tortillas and wrap tightly in foil. Heat in a 350° oven for 10 minutes to soften. (When ready to fill tortillas, remove only *half* at a time, keeping remaining ones warm in oven.) |
| | ● For each flauta, overlap *2* softened tortillas by about half. Spoon about ⅓ *cup* of the chicken mixture lengthwise down center of overlapped tortillas. Roll up tortillas lengthwise as tightly as possible (see photo, right). Secure with wooden toothpicks. |
| Cooking oil | ● In a heavy 10- or 12-inch skillet (or an electric skillet) heat about ½ inch of oil to 365°. Fry rolled up tortillas, 2 or 3 at a time, for 3 to 4 minutes total or till crisp and golden brown. Drain on paper towels. Keep flautas warm in a 300° oven while frying remaining ones. |
| Shredded lettuce<br>Guacamole (see recipe, page 16) *or* frozen avocado dip, thawed<br>Dairy sour cream<br>Homemade Salsa (see recipe, page 36) *or* salsa<br>Hot pepper slices (optional) | ● Remove toothpicks. Serve flautas on shredded lettuce with Guacamole or avocado dip, sour cream, and Homemade Salsa or salsa. Garnish with hot pepper slices, if desired. Serves 4. |

# Top It Off

It would take a mathematical wizard to compute all the different topping combinations for enchiladas, tacos, flautas, tostadas, burritos, or chimichangas. Check out our suggestions—chopped or sliced ripe olives; sliced radishes; chopped chili peppers (fresh, canned, or pickled); chopped tomatoes; finely chopped onion or sliced green onion; and chunks or slices of avocado—or add your own.

Temper the flame from a really hot and spicy combo with a topping of sour cream or mild guacamole, or both. (See our recipe, page 16 or use frozen avocado dip.) And if you want to *add* fuel to the fire, try one of our brightly colored salsas, or a bottled taco sauce or salsa that's labeled *HOT*.

Finally, don't forget lots of shredded cheese to top off your Mexican meal!

# Super Burritos

*Pictured on pages 4–5.*

1 pound ground beef,
    Homemade Chorizo (see
    recipe, page 8), *or*
    bulk chorizo
1 cup chopped onion
½ cup chopped green
    pepper
1 clove garlic, minced
¼ cup water
1 tablespoon chili powder
¼ teaspoon ground cumin
1 cup cooked rice
1 4-ounce can diced green
    chili peppers, drained

● For filling, in a large skillet cook ground beef or chorizo, onion, green pepper, and garlic till meat is brown and onion is tender. Drain off fat.

Stir in water, chili powder, and cumin. Cook about 5 minutes or till most of the water has evaporated. Remove skillet from heat. Stir in rice and *half* of the chili peppers. (Use remaining peppers in Burrito Sauce, below).

**Transform Super Burritos into Super Chimichangas by folding and frying the filled tortillas according to the directions and illustrations in Beef Chimichangas (see recipe, opposite).**

8 10-inch Flour Tortillas
    (see recipe, page 7) *or*
    purchased flour tortillas
1 cup shredded cheddar
    cheese (4 ounces)
1 medium tomato, chopped

● Stack tortillas and wrap tightly in foil. Heat in a 350° oven for 10 minutes to soften. (When ready to fill tortillas, remove only *half* at a time, keeping remaining ones warm in oven.)

Spoon a scant ½ *cup* filling onto *each* tortilla just below center. Top *each* with cheese and tomato. Fold bottom edge of each tortilla up and over filling just till mixture is covered. Fold opposite sides of each tortilla in, just till they meet. Roll up tortillas from the bottom. Secure with wooden toothpicks.

Shredded lettuce
Burrito Sauce
Shredded cheddar cheese
Guacamole (see recipe,
    page 16) *or* frozen
    avocado dip, thawed

● Arrange burritos on a baking sheet. Bake in a 350° oven for 10 to 12 minutes or till heated through.

Remove toothpicks. Serve burritos on lettuce with Burrito Sauce, cheddar cheese, and Guacamole or avocado dip. Makes 4 servings.

**Burrito Sauce:** In a medium saucepan melt 2 tablespoons *butter or margarine.* Stir in 1 tablespoon *all-purpose flour.* Add 1 cup *chicken broth* all at once. Cook and stir over medium heat till thickened and bubbly, then cook and stir 1 minute more. Stir 2 tablespoons *all-purpose flour* into one 8-ounce carton dairy *sour cream.* Stir sour cream and remaining *green chili peppers* into sauce. Cook and stir till thickened and bubbly, then cook and stir for 1 minute more.

# Beef Chimichangas

| | |
|---|---|
| 1 **pound ground beef**<br>½ **cup chopped onion**<br>1 **clove garlic, minced**<br>4 **teaspoons all-purpose flour** | ● For filling, in a large skillet cook ground beef, onion, and garlic till meat is brown and onion is tender. Drain off fat, then stir in flour. |
| 1 **8¾-ounce can whole kernel corn, drained**<br>1 **8-ounce can tomato sauce**<br>1 **7½-ounce can tomatoes, cut up**<br>2 **tablespoons chili powder** | ● Stir corn, tomato sauce, *undrained* tomatoes, and chili powder into meat mixture. Cook and stir till thickened and bubbly. Cook and stir for 1 minute more. |
| 8 **10-inch Flour Tortillas (see recipe, page 7) *or* purchased flour tortillas**<br>1 **cup shredded cheddar *or* American cheese (4 ounces)** | ● Meanwhile, stack tortillas and wrap tightly in foil. Heat in a 350° oven for 10 minutes to soften. (When ready to fill tortillas, remove only *half* at a time, keeping remaining ones warm in oven.)<br><br>Spoon about ⅓ *cup* filling down center of *each* tortilla. Top *each* with about *2 tablespoons* cheese. Fold in the 2 sides envelope fashion (see top illustration, right). Roll up each tortilla, starting from one of the short sides (see middle illustration, right). Secure with wooden toothpicks (see bottom illustration, right). |
| **Cooking oil** | ● In a heavy deep skillet or saucepan heat about 1 inch of oil to 375°. Fry filled tortillas, 2 or 3 at a time, about 1 minute on each side or till crisp and golden brown. Drain on paper towels. Keep chimichangas warm in a 300° oven while frying remaining ones. |
| 2 **cups shredded lettuce**<br>½ **cup shredded carrot**<br>**Green Chili Sauce (see recipe, page 35) *or* one 12-ounce jar green chili salsa**<br>**Dairy sour cream** | ● In a small mixing bowl stir together lettuce and carrot.<br><br>Remove toothpicks. Serve on lettuce-carrot mixture with Green Chili Sauce or salsa and sour cream. Makes 4 servings. |

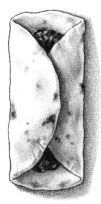

**Fold in the two opposite sides of the tortilla envelope fashion.**

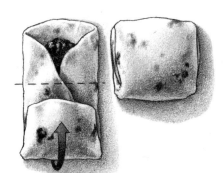

**Carefully roll up the tortilla, starting from one of the short sides.**

**Secure the rolled tortilla with wooden toothpicks.**

# Picadillo Chimichangas

*Pictured on pages 4–5.*

| 6 10-inch Flour Tortillas (see recipe, page 7) or purchased flour tortillas | ● Stack tortillas and wrap tightly in foil. Heat in a 350° oven for 10 minutes to soften. (When ready to fill tortillas, remove only *half* at a time, keeping the remaining ones warm in the oven.) |
|---|---|
| 2 cups Picadillo (see recipe, below)<br>¾ cup shredded Monterey Jack cheese (3 ounces) | ● Spoon about ⅓ cup Picadillo down the center of *each* tortilla. Top *each* with about *2 tablespoons* cheese. Fold opposite sides of the tortilla in over the filling. Fold up the tortilla, starting from one of the short sides. Secure with wooden toothpicks. |
| Cooking oil | ● In a heavy skillet or saucepan heat about 1 inch of oil to 375°. Fry filled tortillas, 2 or 3 at a time, about 1 minute on each side or till crisp and golden brown. Drain on paper towels. Keep chimichangas warm in a 300° oven while frying the remaining ones. |
| Shredded lettuce<br>Ranchero Salsa (see recipe, page 34)<br>1¼ cups shredded Monterey Jack cheese (5 ounces)<br>Guacamole (see recipe, page 16) *or* frozen avocado dip, thawed | ● Remove toothpicks. Serve chimichangas on lettuce with Ranchero Salsa, cheese, and Guacamole or avocado dip. Makes 3 servings. |

Skip the frying and follow these directions for easy oven-fried chimichangas: Brush both sides of the softened flour tortillas with melted *butter or margarine.* Fill the tortillas as directed at left and place in a 15x10x1-inch baking pan. Bake in a 500° oven for 8 to 10 minutes or till golden brown, brushing with additional melted butter or margarine halfway through baking.

# Picadillo

| 1 pound ground beef<br>½ cup chopped onion<br>2 cloves garlic, minced<br>2 medium tomatoes<br>1 medium apple<br>⅓ cup raisins<br>2 tablespoons thinly sliced pimiento-stuffed olives<br>1 tablespoon chopped canned jalapeño pepper<br>1 tablespoon vinegar<br>1 teaspoon sugar<br>½ teaspoon ground cinnamon<br>½ teaspoon ground cumin<br>⅛ teaspoon ground cloves<br>¼ cup toasted slivered almonds | ● In a large skillet cook ground beef, onion, and garlic till meat is brown and onion is tender. Drain off fat.<br><br>Meanwhile, peel and chop tomatoes. Peel, core, and chop apple. Stir tomatoes, apple, raisins, olives, jalapeño pepper, vinegar, sugar, cinnamon, cumin, cloves, and 1 teaspoon *salt* into the beef mixture. Simmer, covered, for 20 minutes. Stir in the toasted almonds. Cook, uncovered, for 2 minutes more. Makes 3 cups. |
|---|---|

A sweet, yet spicy, meat filling, picadillo (pee-kah-DEE-yoh) can double as an hors d'oeuvre. Scoop it up with large corn chip dippers or tortilla chips.

# Chicken Tostadas

*Pictured on pages 4–5.*

| | |
|---|---|
| 2 whole medium chicken breasts (about 1½ pounds total)<br>1 cup water | ● Place chicken breasts in a large skillet. Add water and bring to boiling. Reduce heat and simmer, covered, for 20 to 25 minutes or till chicken is tender. Drain well. Let stand till cool enough to handle.<br>Skin and bone chicken breasts. Use a fork to pull chicken apart into long, thin shreds (you should have about 2¼ cups). Set chicken aside. |
| 2 cups shredded lettuce<br>⅓ cup shredded carrot<br>2 tablespoons salad oil<br>1 tablespoon lemon juice<br>1 tablespoon vinegar | ● Meanwhile, in a medium mixing bowl combine lettuce and carrot. Stir together salad oil, lemon juice, and vinegar, then toss with lettuce mixture. Set aside. |
| Salsa *or* taco sauce<br>1 10½-ounce can jalapeño bean dip<br>1 large avocado, seeded, peeled, and cut up<br>1 tablespoon lemon juice | ● In a small mixing bowl add enough salsa or taco sauce (about ½ cup) to bean dip to make it spreadable.<br>In a small mixing bowl use a fork to mash avocado. Stir in lemon juice. |
| Cooking oil<br>6 6-inch Corn Tortillas (see recipe, page 6) *or* purchased corn tortillas | ● In a heavy skillet heat about ¼ inch of oil. Fry tortillas, 1 at a time, in hot oil about 30 seconds on each side or till crisp and golden brown. Drain on paper towels. Keep tortillas warm in a 300° oven while frying the remaining ones. |
| ¾ cup shredded cheddar *or* Monterey Jack cheese (3 ounces)<br>1 medium tomato, chopped<br>⅓ cup sliced pitted ripe olives | ● Place tortillas on 6 dinner plates. Dividing ingredients equally among tortillas, layer ingredients in the following order: bean dip mixture, avocado, chicken, lettuce mixture, cheese, tomato, and olives. Makes 6 servings. |

**Enjoy the ultimate open-face sandwich. Just mound a crisp corn tortilla high with vegetables, chicken, and cheese.**

# FAJITAS

Assembling your own fajita (fah-HEE-tuh) is like filling a taco. Pile a warm flour tortilla with bite-size strips of chicken or marinated skirt steak, then top with Guacamole, Pico de Gallo Salsa, cheese, and any other condiments you like. Roll it up and you've got yourself a fajita. (By the way, fajita aficionados claim that the chicken or beef *must* be brought to the table sizzling hot or it's not a true South Texas fajita.)

**Spicy-Hot Chicken Fajitas**
*(see recipe, page 19)*

# Sizzling Beef Fajitas

|  |  |
|---|---|
| 1 to 1¼ pounds boneless beef plate skirt steak, flank steak, *or* round steak<br>½ cup Italian salad dressing<br>½ cup salsa<br>2 tablespoons soy sauce | ● Partially freeze beef. Thinly slice across the grain into thin bite-size strips and set aside.<br>For marinade, in a large mixing bowl stir together salad dressing, salsa, and soy sauce. Add beef, stirring to coat. Cover and marinate in the refrigerator for 6 hours or overnight, stirring occasionally. Drain beef well. |
| 8 8-inch Flour Tortillas (see recipe, page 7) *or* purchased flour tortillas | ● Stack tortillas and wrap in foil. Heat in a 350° oven for 10 minutes to soften. |
| 1 tablespoon cooking oil<br>1 small onion, thinly sliced and separated into rings<br>1 medium green pepper, cut into thin strips | ● Meanwhile, preheat a 10-inch skillet over medium-high heat, then add oil (add more oil as necessary during cooking). Cook and stir onion rings in hot oil for 1½ minutes. Add green pepper strips. Cook and stir for 1½ minutes or till vegetables are crisp-tender. Remove vegetables from skillet. |
|  | ● Add *half* of the beef to the hot skillet. Cook and stir for 2 to 3 minutes or till done. Remove beef. Cook and stir remaining beef for 2 to 3 minutes. Drain well. Return all beef and vegetables to skillet. Cook and stir for 1 to 2 minutes or till heated through. |
| Guacamole (see recipe, page 16) *or* frozen avocado dip, thawed<br>Pico de Gallo Salsa (see recipe, page 35)<br>Dairy sour cream<br>Shredded cheddar cheese | ● To serve, immediately fill warmed tortillas with beef-vegetable mixture, then add Guacamole or avocado dip, Pico de Gallo Salsa, sour cream, and cheese, as desired. Roll fajitas up. Makes 4 servings. |

**Guacamole:** In a blender container or food processor bowl combine 2 medium *avocados*, seeded, peeled, and cut up; 1 medium *tomato*, peeled, seeded, and coarsely chopped; ½ small *onion*, cut up; 1 tablespoon chopped *serrano or jalapeño pepper*; 1 tablespoon snipped *cilanto or parsley*; 1 tablespoon *lemon or lime juice*; and ¼ teaspoon *salt*.

Cover and blend or process till well combined, stopping machine occasionally to scrape down sides. Transfer mixture to a serving bowl. Cover and chill. Use as a dip for chips or as a topper for main dishes. Makes about 1¾ cups.

# Spicy-Hot Chicken Fajitas

*Pictured on pages 16–17.*

| | |
|---|---|
| 3 whole medium chicken breasts (about 2¼ pounds total), skinned and boned<br>½ cup hot-style tomato juice *or* tomato juice<br>1 to 2 tablespoons chopped canned jalapeño peppers<br>2 teaspoons cornstarch<br>½ teaspoon instant chicken bouillon granules | ● Cut chicken into thin bite-size strips and set aside.<br>  For sauce, in a small mixing bowl stir together tomato juice, jalapeño peppers, cornstarch, and bouillon granules. Set sauce mixture aside. |
| 8 8-inch Flour Tortillas (see recipe, page 7) *or* purchased flour tortillas | ● Stack tortillas and wrap in foil. Heat in a 350° oven for 10 minutes to soften. |
| 1 tablespoon cooking oil<br>1 small zucchini, cut into 2-inch-long julienne strips (about 1½ cups)<br>3 green onions, bias-sliced into 1-inch lengths (about ½ cup) | ● Meanwhile, preheat a 10-inch skillet over medium-high heat, then add oil (add more oil as necessary during cooking). Cook and stir zucchini in hot oil for 30 seconds. Add onion and cook and stir for 1½ minutes or till vegetables are crisp-tender. Remove from skillet. |
| | ● Add *half* of the chicken to the hot skillet. Cook and stir for 2 to 3 minutes or till done. Remove chicken. Cook and stir remaining chicken for 2 to 3 minutes. Return all chicken to skillet. Push the chicken from the center of the skillet. |
| 1 medium tomato, cut into thin wedges | ● Stir sauce, then add to the center of skillet. Cook and stir till thickened and bubbly, then cook and stir for 1 minute more. Return vegetables to skillet. Stir ingredients together to coat with sauce. Arrange tomato atop. Cover and cook for 1 minute. |
| Guacamole (see recipe, page 16) *or* frozen avocado dip, thawed<br>Pico de Gallo Salsa (see recipe, page 35)<br>Dairy sour cream<br>Shredded cheddar cheese | ● To serve, immediately fill warmed tortillas with chicken-vegetable mixture, then add Guacamole or avocado dip, Pico de Gallo Salsa, sour cream, and cheese, as desired. Roll fajitas up. Makes 4 servings. |

**Once you've tried the traditional *beef* fajitas, branch out and sink your teeth into a couple of these surprisingly spicy *chicken* fajitas.**

# New Mexican Enchiladas

*Also pictured on the cover.*

|  |  |
|---|---|
| ¾ **pound ground beef**<br>½ **cup chopped onion**<br>1 **clove garlic, minced** | ● In a medium skillet cook ground beef, onion, and garlic till beef is brown and onion is tender. Drain well. |
| **Picante Sauce (see recipe, page 34)**<br>¾ **cup sliced pitted ripe olives** | ● Stir *1 cup* Picante Sauce and olives into meat mixture. Cook and stir over low heat about 5 minutes or till most of the liquid has evaporated. Set aside. |
| 2 **tablespoons cooking oil**<br>6 **6-inch Corn Tortillas (see recipe, page 6)** *or* **purchased corn tortillas** | ● In a heavy skillet heat cooking oil. Dip tortillas, 1 at a time, in hot oil for 10 seconds or just till limp, adding more oil if needed. Drain on paper towels. |
| 1 **cup shredded cheddar cheese (4 ounces)** | ● To assemble first stack, place a spoonful of Picante Sauce on an ovenproof plate. Top with a tortilla, about ¼ *cup* meat mixture, and *2 tablespoons* cheese. Repeat layers twice more. On a second ovenproof plate, repeat to assemble a second stack. |
| 2 **fried eggs** | ● Pour about ¼ *cup* of the remaining Picante Sauce over *each* enchilada stack and sprinkle with remaining cheese. Cover loosely with foil. Put plates into a 350° oven for 10 minutes or till heated through. Remove from oven and top each stack with a fried egg. Serve with remaining Picante Sauce. Serves 4. |

**When you don't want to fry the eggs, serve these enchiladas as they're pictured on the cover. Arrange shredded lettuce around the stacks and top with the remaining Picante Sauce and sour cream. Garnish with hot pepper flowers.**

# Chicken Enchiladas With Green Sauce

*Pictured on pages 4–5.*

| | |
|---|---|
| 3 poblano *or* Anaheim peppers, *or* one 4-ounce can diced green chili peppers, drained | ● If using fresh peppers, loosen skins by broiling peppers 4 inches from heat till charred on all sides, turning once. Place the charred peppers in a paper bag. Close the bag tightly and let stand 10 minutes. Remove peppers from bag. Peel skin away from flesh and cut off stems. Slit peppers open and scrape away seeds and ribs. Coarsely chop peppers. (See page 30.) Set peppers aside to use in Green Sauce. |
| 2 tablespoons cooking oil<br>8 6-inch Corn Tortillas (see recipe, page 6) *or* purchased corn tortillas | ● Meanwhile, in a heavy skillet heat oil. Dip tortillas, 1 at a time, in hot oil for 10 seconds or just till limp, adding more oil if needed. Drain on paper towels. |
| 2 cups chopped cooked chicken *or* turkey<br>Green Sauce | ● Spoon about ¼ *cup* chicken onto *each* tortilla, then roll up. Place the filled tortillas, seam side down, in a 10x6x2-inch baking dish. Top with Green Sauce. |
| ½ cup shredded Monterey Jack cheese (2 ounces)<br>Snipped cilantro *or* parsley (optional)<br>Sliced radishes (optional)<br>Chopped onion (optional) | ● Bake, covered, in a 350° oven for 15 to 20 minutes or till heated through. Remove foil and top with cheese. Return to oven and bake for 1 to 2 minutes more or till cheese melts. Garnish with cilantro or parsley, radishes, and onion, if desired. Makes 4 servings. |

**Green Sauce:** In a blender container or food processor bowl place fresh or canned peppers; one 13-ounce can *tomatillos,* drained and rinsed; 1 small *onion,* cut up; 2 sprigs *cilantro or parsley;* and 1 clove *garlic.* Cover and blend or process till almost smooth.

Transfer sauce mixture to a small saucepan. Stir in ½ cup *chicken broth,* 1 teaspoon *sugar,* ⅛ teaspoon *salt,* and dash *pepper.* Bring to boiling. Reduce heat and simmer, covered, 10 minutes.

Mexican cooks have been serving sauces like this Green Sauce for centuries, especially with poultry. So take a tip from our Mexican neighbors—make up a double batch and serve some (along with taco sauce) on chicken tacos or tostadas.

# Creamy Seafood Enchiladas

1 8-ounce package cream cheese, softened
½ cup shredded Monterey Jack cheese (2 ounces)
2 tablespoons dry white wine
2 6-ounce packages frozen crab meat and shrimp, thawed and drained

● For filling, in a small mixer bowl combine cream cheese, Monterey Jack cheese, and wine. Beat with an electric mixer till almost smooth. Stir in crab meat and shrimp.

2 tablespoons cooking oil
12 6-inch Corn Tortillas (see recipe, page 6) or purchased corn tortillas

● In a heavy skillet heat cooking oil. Dip tortillas, 1 at a time, in hot oil for 10 seconds or just till limp, adding more oil if needed. Drain on paper towels.

● Spoon about ¼ cup filling onto each tortilla, then roll up. Place the filled tortillas, seam side down, in a 13x9x2-inch baking dish.

½ cup sliced green onion
3 tablespoons butter or margarine
¼ cup all-purpose flour
¼ teaspoon salt
¼ teaspoon pepper
2¾ cups milk

● For sauce, in a medium saucepan cook onion in butter or margarine till tender but not brown. Stir in flour, salt, and pepper. Add milk all at once. Cook and stir till thickened and bubbly. Pour sauce over tortillas.

1 cup shredded Monterey Jack cheese (4 ounces)
Sliced green onion
Paprika

● Bake, covered, in a 350° oven for 15 to 20 minutes or till heated through. Remove foil and top with cheese. Return to oven and bake about 5 minutes more or till cheese melts. Garnish with green onion and paprika. Makes 6 servings.

*Milk* to put out a hot pepper fire? The oils that give hot peppers their zip dissolve in fat. So a swig of whole milk works better than skim milk, pop, or even water at dousing a hot pepper fire in your mouth. Another sure-fire remedy is beer—hot pepper oils also dissolve in alcohol.

Spread dough so one of the long sides is at the long edge of the wrapper. Leave equal space at both ends (with the irregular shape of cornhusks, the space at both ends may not be quite equal). Spoon filling down center.

# Classic Tamales

| | |
|---|---|
| 12  cornhusks *or* foil *or* parchment paper rectangles | ● For wrappers, soak cornhusks in warm water several hours or overnight to soften. Pat with paper towels to remove excess moisture. (*Or,* cut foil or parchment into 8x6-inch rectangles.) |
| Tamale Dough (see recipe, page 26) | ● Spoon a scant ¼ *cup* of dough onto *each* tamale wrapper. Spread dough into a 5x4-inch rectangle, spreading 1 long side of dough to edge of wrapper and leaving equal spaces at both ends. |
| Tamale Filling (see recipe, page 26) | ● Spoon tamale filling lengthwise down center of dough, bringing filling out to both ends. Fold long edge of wrapper *over* filling so it overlaps dough about ½ inch, then continue rolling up wrapper jelly-roll style. Seal ends securely (see photo, right). |
| | ● Place tamales on a steamer basket in an electric skillet. Add water to just below basket level, then bring to boiling. Cover and steam tamales at medium heat for 45 to 50 minutes or till tamales pull away from wrappers. (Add more water as necessary.) Unwrap tamales and serve immediately. Makes 12 tamales. |

When you're using a foil wrapper, fold the ends underneath. For parchment paper or cornhusk wrappers, twist the ends and tie with string to seal.

Fold the long edge of the wrapper *over* the filling so it overlaps dough about ½ inch. Continue rolling up wrapper jelly-roll style. Tie ends with pieces of cornhusk or string.

Steam tamales in an electric skillet (as shown) or use a Chinese steamer basket over a wok or saucepan. Remember to add boiling water to the skillet, wok, or saucepan as necessary, but avoid peeking, as this lets steam escape.

# Savory Chicken Tamales

*Pictured on pages 24–25.*

| | |
|---|---|
| 12 **cornhusks** *or* **foil** *or* **parchment paper rectangles** | ● For wrappers, soak cornhusks in warm water several hours or overnight to soften. Pat with paper towels to remove excess moisture. (*Or,* cut foil or parchment into 8x6-inch rectangles.) |
| 2¼ **cups Masa Harina tortilla flour**<br>1 **cup warm water**<br>¾ **cup shortening** *or* **lard**<br>¼ **teaspoon salt** | ● For tamale dough, in a large mixing bowl stir together tortilla flour and water. Cover and let stand 20 minutes.<br>    In a large mixer bowl beat together shortening or lard and salt till fluffy. Beat in flour mixture till well combined. |
| | ● Spoon a scant *¼ cup* dough onto *each* tamale wrapper. Spread dough into a 5x4-inch rectangle, spreading 1 long side of the dough to the edge of the wrapper and leaving equal spaces at both ends (see photo, pages 24–25). |
| **Red Chili Sauce (see recipe, page 35)** *or* **Picante Sauce (see recipe, page 34)**<br>1 **cup finely chopped cooked chicken** | ● Spoon a scant *1 tablespoon* Red Chili Sauce or Picante Sauce lengthwise down the center of dough, bringing sauce out to both ends (see photo, pages 24–25). Top with about *1 tablespoon* chicken. |
| | ● Fold long edge of wrapper *over* filling so it overlaps dough about ½ inch, then continue rolling up wrapper jelly-roll style. Tie ends securely with pieces of cornhusk or string. *Or,* for foil, fold ends under to seal. (See photo, pages 24–25.) |
| | ● Place tamales on a steamer basket in an electric skillet. Add water to just below the basket level, then bring to boiling. Cover and steam tamales at medium heat for 35 to 40 minutes or till tamales pull away from wrappers. (Add more water as necessary.)<br>    Unwrap tamales. Serve immediately with remaining warm Red Chili Sauce or Picante Sauce. Makes 12 tamales. |

**Tamales are "fiesta food" in Mexico. Filled with meat, they make a hearty meal, but stuff them with sweets, and they're an irresistible dessert or between-meal snack.**

# Sweet Tamales With Lemon Sauce

| | |
|---|---|
| 16 **cornhusks** *or* **foil** *or* **parchment paper rectangles** | ● For wrappers, soak cornhusks in warm water several hours or overnight to soften. Pat with paper towels to remove excess moisture. (*Or,* cut foil or parchment into 8x6-inch rectangles.) |

| | |
|---|---|
| 2¼ **cups Masa Harina tortilla flour** <br> 1 **cup orange juice** <br> ¼ **cup dry white wine** *or* **water** <br> ¾ **cup shortening** *or* **lard** <br> ⅓ **cup sugar** <br> ¼ **teaspoon ground cinnamon** <br> ⅛ **teaspoon ground nutmeg** | ● For tamale dough, in a large mixing bowl stir together tortilla flour, orange juice, and wine or water. Cover and let stand 20 minutes. <br><br> In a large mixer bowl beat together shortening or lard, sugar, cinnamon, and nutmeg till fluffy. Beat in flour mixture till well combined. |

| | |
|---|---|
| ¾ **cup raisins** <br> ¾ **cup mixed dried fruit bits** <br> ⅓ **cup rum** <br> 1½ **cups coconut** <br> ¼ **cup chopped pecans** *or* **walnuts** | ● In a small mixing bowl combine raisins, fruit bits, and rum. Let stand 20 minutes. Drain fruit mixture, reserving liquid. Stir coconut and nuts into fruit mixture, adding as much of the reserved liquid as necessary to moisten. |

| | |
|---|---|
| | ● Spoon a scant *¼ cup* of dough onto *each* tamale wrapper. Spread dough into a 5x4-inch rectangle, spreading 1 long side of the dough to the edge of the wrapper and leaving equal spaces at both ends (see photo, pages 24–25). |

| | |
|---|---|
| | ● Spoon about *3 tablespoons* fruit mixture lengthwise down the center of the dough, bringing the mixture out to both ends (see photo, pages 24–25). <br><br> Fold long edge of wrapper *over* filling so it overlaps dough about ½ inch, then continue rolling up wrapper jelly-roll style. Tie ends securely with pieces of cornhusks or string. *Or,* for foil, fold ends under to seal. (See photo, pages 24–25.) |

| | |
|---|---|
| 4 **cups peeled and sliced kiwi fruit, cantaloupe,** *or* **peaches; sliced apples** *or* **pears; raspberries** *or* **blueberries;** *and/or* **halved strawberries** <br> **Lemon Sauce (see recipe, right)** | ● Place tamales on a steamer basket in an electric skillet. Add water to just below the basket level, then bring to boiling. Cover and steam tamales at medium heat for 35 to 40 minutes or till tamales pull away from wrappers. (Add more water as necessary.) <br><br> Unwrap tamales. Serve immediately with desired fruit and Lemon Sauce. Makes 16 tamales. |

**Lemon Sauce:** In a medium saucepan combine ⅓ cup *sugar,* 1 tablespoon *cornstarch,* and a dash of ground *nutmeg.* Stir in 1 cup *water.* Cook and stir till thickened and bubbly, then cook and stir 1 minute more.

Stir about ½ *cup* of the hot mixture into 1 beaten *egg yolk.* Return all to saucepan. Cook and stir till bubbly, then cook and stir 1 minute more. Remove from heat and stir in 1 tablespoon *butter or margarine,* ¼ teaspoon *finely shredded lemon peel,* and 1 tablespoon *lemon juice.* Makes about 1⅓ cups.

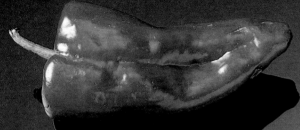

**Chipotle pepper**
*(dried; very hot)*

**Cascabel pepper**
*(dried; medium-hot to hot)*

**Poblano pepper**
*(fresh; mild to medium-hot)*

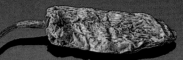

**Guajillo pepper**
*(dried; very hot)*

**De árbol pepper**
*(dried; very hot)*

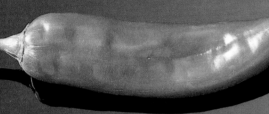

**Anaheim pepper**
*(fresh; mild)*

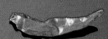

**Cayenne pepper**
*(dried; very hot)*

**Ancho pepper**
*(dried; mild to medium-hot)*

**Pequin pepper**
*(dried; very, very hot)*

**Jalapeño pepper**
*(fresh; hot to very hot)*

**Mulato pepper**
*(dried; medium hot)*

**Pequin pepper**
*(fresh; very, very hot)*

**Serrano pepper**
*(fresh; very hot)*

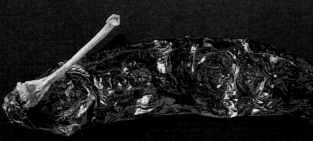

**Pasilla pepper**
*(dried; very hot)*

# Chili Pepper Identification

When you first explore Mexican cuisine, the subject of chili peppers can be rather confusing. There are dozens of varieties of peppers, each with its own characteristics. And to make matters more confusing, different regions have different names for the same pepper. In addition, many peppers are called by one name when they're fresh and another when they're dried.

Look for chili peppers in Mexican groceries, gourmet food stores, and many large supermarkets, but keep in mind that not every pepper is available at all times. And remember, you can substitute one pepper for another if they have similar traits.

So, check the photo, opposite and the chart at right for the low-down on fresh and dried peppers. They will simplify the task of shopping for and cooking with these Mexican flavor secrets.

Fresh **Anaheim peppers** (also called California green chili peppers) are light green in color. These firm and thick-fleshed peppers are 4 to 6 inches long and about 1½ inches wide, with a rounded tip. Anaheim peppers have a mild flavor with just a slight bite—they're seldom hot. Fresh as well as canned whole or diced Anaheims are widely available in American supermarkets.

The most common of the dried peppers is the **ancho** (which is a dried poblano). Like poblanos, anchos are large and triangular, with wrinkled dark reddish-brown skin. They range from mild to medium-hot. Ancho peppers are the heart of many red chili sauces, as well as a major ingredient in commercial chili powders. In most cases, if ancho peppers aren't available, you can substitute 1 tablespoon of chili powder for each pepper.

Dried **cascabel** peppers range from medium-hot to hot. They're small and round, with a fairly smooth, dark red skin.

The small, narrow, red **cayenne** pepper virtually breathes fire. It's used almost exclusively in its ground form and is simply called ground red pepper.

**Chipotle** peppers are smoked and dried jalapeño peppers. They have a dull brown, wrinkled skin and a rich, smoky, hot flavor.

The dried **de árbol** pepper is small and slender, with a very hot flavor. Its skin is a smooth, bright red.

Very hot, dried **guajillo** peppers are medium-size with a long, narrow shape and a fairly smooth, dark reddish-brown skin.

The famous **jalapeño** pepper is small—2½ to 3 inches long and ¾ to 1 inch wide. You can easily recognize this fresh dark green pepper by its blunt or slightly tapered end. Its flavor varies from hot to very hot. Jalapeños are available whole and sliced, canned and pickled.

The dried **mulato** is a large, triangular pepper that has wrinkled, blackish-brown skin. It is pungent and medium-hot.

Dried **pasilla** peppers, sometimes known as "negro chilies," are long, slender, medium-size peppers with wrinkled, blackish-brown skins. The pungent flavor of the pasilla pepper is usually very hot. It's often used in combination with ancho peppers.

The tiny, round or oval-shape **pequin** pepper is very, very hot. Dried pequin peppers have a slightly wrinkled, orangish-red skin. You'll sometimes see these peppers labeled "tepin chili peppers."

The fresh, dark green **poblano** is a large, plump, bell-shape pepper, with a pointed end. Poblanos usually range in length from 3½ to 5 inches and their flavor varies from mild to medium-hot. These peppers are stuffed whole to make the classic Chiles Rellenos (see our recipe, page 57).

The small, but mighty, fresh **serrano** pepper is only 1 to 1½ inches long and ⅜ inch wide, with a pointed end. Usually dark green, but sometimes allowed to ripen to red, the serrano is very hot. It's available canned and pickled.

# Working with Chili Peppers

### What's Hot?
A common fallacy is that the seeds are the hottest part of a pepper. But most of the fire is actually in the membrane and ribs. So for milder flavor, remove membranes, ribs, and seeds before using.

### Handling Chili Peppers
Because chili peppers contain oils that burn skin and eyes, avoid direct contact with the peppers as much as possible. When working with peppers, wear plastic or rubber gloves or work under cold running water. If your bare hands touch the chili peppers, wash your hands and nails well with soap and water.

### Preparing Dried Chili Peppers
Most recipes require that dried chili peppers be soaked till soft and then puréed. To soften, rinse the dried chili peppers in water. Cut them open and discard the stems and seeds. Cut the peppers into small pieces with a knife or scissors, as shown above. Soak them in boiling water for 45 to 60 minutes or till they're pliable. Drain well and continue as recipe directs.

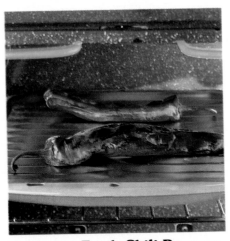

### Preparing Fresh Chili Peppers
It's often best to peel the skin from fresh peppers before using them. (This is not necessary, however, when chopping or slicing small amounts of fresh jalapeño or serrano peppers.)

To loosen the skin for easier peeling, place peppers on a broiler pan 4 inches from heat, as shown above. Broil, turning often, till the peppers are charred on all sides. Place the broiled peppers in a paper bag. Close the bag tightly and let stand 10 minutes. This steams the peppers so the skin peels away easily.

Cut the stems off the peppers. To remove seeds and ribs, slit the peppers open and place seed side up on a flat surface. Use a knife to scrape seeds and ribs from the flesh, as shown at right. Slice or chop as directed in recipe.

### Storing Chili Peppers
Dried chili peppers will keep in a cool, dry place for up to a year. For longer storage, freeze them in an airtight container.

Store fresh peppers in paper bags in the refrigerator for up to one week. Or, roast the peppers, cool, and freeze them in plastic bags (The skins will peel off easily as the peppers thaw.)

### Using Canned Chili Peppers
Rinse both plain and pickled canned chili peppers before using to remove the salty packing liquid.

To remove the seeds from whole chili peppers, slit them open and use a knife to scrape out the seeds and ribs, as you would for fresh chili peppers. Chop or slice the chili peppers as directed in the recipe.

# Jalapeño Nachos

4 cups tortilla chips
1 cup Refried Beans (see recipe, page 87) *or* ½ of a 16-ounce can refried beans
¼ cup Picante Sauce (see recipe, page 34) *or* salsa

● Arrange chips about one layer deep (overlapping slightly) on an 11- or 12-inch ovenproof platter. In a small saucepan combine refried beans and Picante Sauce or salsa. Cook and stir just till heated through. Immediately spoon bean mixture over chips.

1 medium tomato, chopped
2 tablespoons to ¼ cup chopped jalapeño peppers
¾ cup shredded Monterey Jack cheese (3 ounces)
¾ cup shredded cheddar cheese (3 ounces)

● Sprinkle tomato and jalapeño peppers evenly over chips. Top with cheeses.
  Bake in a 425° oven for 2 to 3 minutes or till cheese melts. Serve immediately. Makes 8 servings.

**Meaty Nachos:** Cook ½ pound *ground beef,* *Homemade Chorizo* (see recipe, page 8), *or bulk chorizo* till brown. Drain well. Stir in ⅓ cup *Picante Sauce or salsa* and heat through. Arrange tortilla chips on an ovenproof platter as directed at left. Drizzle meat mixture over chips. Top with 1½ cups shredded *cheddar or American cheese.* Bake as directed at left.

# Cheese Crisps

*Pictured on page 33.*

1 cup all-purpose flour
½ teaspoon baking powder
¼ teaspoon salt
1½ teaspoons shortening *or* lard
¼ to ⅓ cup warm water (110° to 115°)

● For tortillas, in a medium mixing bowl stir together flour, baking powder, and salt. Cut in shortening or lard till thoroughly combined. Gradually add warm water and toss together till dough can be gathered into a ball (if necessary, add more water, 1 teaspoon at a time). Knead dough 15 to 20 times. Let dough rest 15 minutes. Divide dough in half and shape into balls.

● On a lightly floured surface, use a rolling pin to flatten each ball of dough into a 10-inch circle. Place the 2 tortillas on lightly greased baking sheets or pizza pans. Bake in a 350° oven for 15 to 20 minutes or till crisp and lightly browned.

1 cup shredded Monterey Jack cheese (4 ounces)
1 cup shredded cheddar cheese (4 ounces)
1 medium tomato, chopped
3 tablespoons sliced green onion
2 tablespoons diced canned green chili peppers, drained

● Sprinkle cheeses evenly over the 2 tortillas. Top each with tomato, onion, and chili peppers. Bake about 5 minutes more or till cheese is bubbly. Remove from oven and cut into wedges. Makes 2.

**When time runs short, make these appetizer Mexican-style pizzas with a couple of packaged 10-inch flour tortillas.**
  **Crisp them in a 350° oven about 8 minutes, sprinkle with toppings, and bake 5 minutes more.**

# Marinated Seafood

| | |
|---|---|
| 8 ounces large fresh *or* frozen peeled and deveined shrimp<br>8 ounces fresh *or* frozen scallops | ● Thaw shrimp and scallops, if frozen. Cut any large scallops in half.<br>    In a medium saucepan cook shrimp and scallops in boiling water about 1 minute or till shrimp turns pink and scallops are opaque. Drain and rinse under cool water to stop cooking. |
| ½ cup lime *or* lemon juice<br>¼ cup water | ● Put shrimp and scallops into a plastic bag, then set bag in a bowl.<br>    For marinade, stir together lime or lemon juice and water. Pour marinade over seafood in bag. Close bag tightly, then turn to evenly distribute the marinade. Chill for 8 hours or overnight, turning bag occasionally. |
| ¼ cup sliced green onion<br>1 4-ounce can diced green chili peppers, drained<br>3 tablespoons olive oil *or* cooking oil<br>1 to 2 tablespoons snipped cilantro *or* parsley<br>1 tablespoon capers, drained | ● Drain shrimp and scallops, discarding marinade. In a medium mixing bowl stir together green onion, chili peppers, oil, cilantro or parsley, capers, dash *salt*, and dash *pepper*. Gently stir in shrimp and scallops till combined. Cover and chill at least 2 hours. |
| 1 medium tomato, seeded and chopped (optional)<br>4 thin slices red onion, halved | ● Just before serving, toss tomato with seafood mixture, if desired. Arrange halved onion slices around edge of serving platter. (Place rounded edge of onion out.) Spoon seafood mixture into center. Makes 6 servings. |

Make individual servings of this first-course appetizer by arranging *4* halved onion slices around the edges of each of *6* individual plates. Spoon some of the seafood mixture into center, then garnish with thin avocado slices and lime wedges, if you like.

# Cheese Quesadillas

| | |
|---|---|
| 2 cups shredded Monterey Jack, cheddar, Swiss, *or* mozzarella cheese<br>6 8-inch Flour Tortillas (see recipe, page 7) *or* purchased flour tortillas<br>1 4-ounce can diced green chili peppers, drained | ● Sprinkle ⅓ *cup* cheese on half of *each* tortilla. Top with chili peppers. Fold tortillas in half, pressing down gently.<br>    In a large skillet or griddle cook tortillas, 2 at a time, over medium-high heat about 4 minutes total or till cheese melts, turning once. Remove tortillas from skillet or griddle and keep warm. |
| Guacamole (see recipe, page 16)<br>Sliced pitted ripe olives<br>Homemade Salsa (see recipe, page 36) (optional) | ● Cut tortillas into 3 triangles. Serve with Guacamole, olives, and Homemade Salsa, if desired. Makes 6 servings. |

Chorizo and Cheese Quesadillas: Prepare as directed at left *except,* using a total of ½ pound *Homemade Chorizo* (see recipe, page 8) *or bulk chorizo,* cooked and drained, sprinkle a little over half of *each* tortilla. Sprinkle 1 cup shredded *cheddar cheese* over chorizo. Fold tortillas in half. Cook and serve as directed at left.

**Cheese Quesadillas**

**Cheese Crisps**
*(see recipe, page 31)*

**Marinated Seafood**

# Ranchero Salsa

| | |
|---|---|
| 2 slices bacon | ● In a medium skillet cook bacon till crisp. Drain, reserving drippings. Crumble bacon and set aside. |
| ½ cup chopped onion<br>1 clove garlic, minced<br>3 medium tomatoes, seeded and chopped (about 2 cups)<br>1 canned jalapeño pepper, drained, seeded, and chopped<br>¼ teaspoon sugar<br>¼ teaspoon ground cumin | ● Cook onion and garlic in reserved drippings till tender but not brown. Stir in tomatoes, jalapeño pepper, sugar, and cumin. Cover and cook over medium heat for 3 minutes. Uncover and simmer for 10 minutes or till most of the liquid has evaporated. Stir in bacon.<br>  Store, tightly covered, in refrigerator for up to 3 days. Use as a topper for main dishes. Makes about 1⅓ cups. |

**Besides Huevos Rancheros, (see recipe, page 57), spoon Ranchero Salsa over scrambled eggs, meat loaf, or a cheese soufflé.**

# Picante Sauce

| | |
|---|---|
| 4 medium tomatoes, seeded and cut up<br>1 medium onion, cut up<br>2 cloves garlic<br>1 to 2 jalapeño *or* serrano peppers<br>2 tablespoons snipped cilantro *or* parsley<br>1 teaspoon celery seed | ● Place tomatoes in a blender container or food processor bowl. Cover and blend or process till coarsely ground. Add onion, garlic, jalapeño or serrano peppers, cilantro or parsley, and celery seed. Cover and blend or process till finely ground. |
| 1 medium green pepper, finely chopped<br>2 tablespoons vinegar<br>1 teaspoon salt<br>1 teaspoon sugar<br>½ teaspoon dried oregano, crushed<br>⅛ teaspoon ground cumin | ● Transfer tomato mixture to a medium saucepan. Stir in green pepper, vinegar, salt, sugar, oregano, and cumin. Bring tomato mixture to boiling. Reduce heat and simmer, uncovered, for 30 to 40 minutes or to desired consistency. |
| | ● Store, tightly covered, in refrigerator for up to 2 weeks. Use as a dip for chips or a topper for main dishes. Makes about 2⅔ cups sauce. |

**Use this fiery sauce like barbecue sauce and brush it onto ribs or burgers during the last 10 to 15 minutes of grilling.**

# Red Chili Sauce *Pictured on page 37.*

| | | |
|---|---|---|
| 6 dried ancho peppers *or* ¼ cup chili powder<br>2 tablespoons cooking oil | ● If using dried peppers, cut open and discard stems and seeds. Cut peppers into small pieces. Place in a bowl and cover with boiling water. Let stand 45 to 60 minutes or till pliable. Drain well. (See page 30.) *Or,* if using chili powder, cook and stir chili powder in hot oil over medium-low heat for 4 minutes. (Omit oil if using dried peppers.) | *Molcajete and Tejolote.* **Sound like a comedy team? It's really the three-legged Mexican version of a mortar and pestle (pictured on page 37). Mexican cooks still prepare thick and chunky guacamoles and salsas with these volcanic rock tools just as they did 3,500 years ago.** |
| 1 14½-ounce can tomatoes<br>2 cloves garlic<br>2 teaspoons sugar<br>½ teaspoon salt<br>½ teaspoon dried oregano, crushed<br>¼ teaspoon ground cumin | ● Place *undrained* tomatoes in a blender container or food processor bowl. Add drained peppers or chili powder mixture and garlic. Cover and blend or process till smooth. Transfer to a saucepan. Stir in sugar, salt, oregano, and cumin. Bring to boiling. Reduce heat and simmer, uncovered, for 10 minutes or till slightly thickened.<br>   Store, tightly covered, in refrigerator for up to 2 weeks. Serve warm as a topper for main dishes. Makes 1½ cups. | |

# Green Chili Sauce

| | | |
|---|---|---|
| ¼ cup chopped onion<br>1 clove garlic, minced<br>1 tablespoon cooking oil<br>3 medium tomatoes, peeled and chopped<br>1 4-ounce can diced green chili peppers, drained<br>1 tablespoon snipped cilantro *or* parsley | ● In a medium skillet cook onion and garlic in hot oil till onion is tender but not brown. Stir in tomatoes, chili peppers, cilantro or parsley, ¼ teaspoon *salt,* and dash *pepper.* Simmer for 10 to 15 minutes or till slightly thickened.<br>   Store, tightly covered, in refrigerator for up to 3 days. Serve warm as a topper for main dishes. Makes about 1½ cups. | **Take a tip from our Test Kitchen: Before peeling a tomato, spear it with a fork and plunge it into boiling water for 20 to 30 seconds. Immediately dip it in cold water—the peel slips right off.** |

# Pico de Gallo Salsa

| | | |
|---|---|---|
| 2 medium tomatoes, peeled and finely chopped<br>2 tablespoons finely chopped onion<br>2 tablespoons snipped cilantro *or* parsley<br>1 serrano pepper, finely chopped<br>Dash sugar | ● In a medium mixing bowl stir together chopped tomatoes, onion, cilantro or parsley, serrano pepper, and sugar. Cover and chill for several hours or overnight, stirring occasionally.<br>   Store, tightly covered, in refrigerator up to 3 days. Use as a dip for chips or a topper for main dishes. Makes 1¼ cups. | **Nobody knows how this salsa inherited its name since Pico de Gallo (PEE-koh day GAH-yoh) is also the name for a traditional Latin American jicama and orange salad.**<br>   **The name, which means "rooster's beak," refers to the old-style way of eating the salad by picking up chunks with your fingers—the way a rooster pecks corn.** |

# Salsa Verde

5 *or* 6 fresh tomatillos, finely chopped, *or* one 13-ounce can tomatillos, drained, rinsed, and finely chopped
2 tablespoons finely chopped onion
1 serrano *or* jalapeño pepper, seeded and finely chopped
1 teaspoon snipped cilantro *or* parsley
¼ teaspoon salt

● In a small mixing bowl stir together tomatillos, onion, serrano or jalapeño pepper, cilantro or parsley, and salt. Cover and chill for several hours or overnight, stirring occasionally.

Store, tightly covered, in the refrigerator for up to 2 days. Use as a dip for chips or as a topper for main dishes. Makes about ¾ cup sauce.

**Tomatillos and fresh cilantro lend their distinctive flavors to this green sauce. Try it over chicken or pork tacos.**

# Homemade Salsa

3 medium tomatoes, peeled and finely chopped (about 2 cups)
1 4-ounce can diced green chili peppers, drained
¼ cup sliced green onion
¼ cup chopped green pepper
2 tablespoons lemon juice
1 to 2 tablespoons snipped cilantro *or* parsley
1 clove garlic, minced
⅛ teaspoon pepper
½ cup tomato sauce

● In a medium mixing bowl stir together tomatoes, chili peppers, green onion, green pepper, lemon juice, cilantro or parsley, garlic, and pepper.

Place about *1 cup* of the tomato mixture and tomato sauce in a blender container or food processor bowl. Cover and blend or process just till pureed. Stir into remaining tomato mixture. Cover and chill for several hours or overnight, stirring occasionally.

Store, tightly covered, in the refrigerator for up to 3 days. Use as a dip for chips or as a topper for main dishes. Makes about 3⅓ cups sauce.

**Salsas are the salt and pepper of Mexico and the American Southwest. No table is set without several bowls of salsa, ranging from mild to searing. (You'll find ours falls in the middle range.) Use it on everything from soups to nachos.**

Red Chili Sauce
*(see recipe, page 35)*

Salsa Verde

Homemade Salsa

# Corn Soup

| | |
|---|---|
| **3 fresh ears of corn *or* one 10-ounce package frozen whole kernel corn, thawed** | ● If using fresh corn, use a sharp knife to cut off just the kernel tips. Then scrape the cob with a knife. (See photo, right.) You should have about 2 cups. |
| **2 medium tomatoes, peeled, seeded, and cut up** | ● In a blender container or food processor bowl combine *half* of the corn (including the milky liquid) and *all* the tomatoes. Cover and blend or process till smooth, stopping machine occasionally to scrape down sides. Set corn-tomato mixture aside. |
| **¼ cup chopped onion**<br>**1 clove garlic, minced**<br>**1 tablespoon butter *or* margarine**<br>**1 cup chicken broth**<br>**¼ teaspoon salt**<br>**⅛ teaspoon pepper**<br>**Several dashes bottled hot pepper sauce (optional)**<br>**½ cup whipping cream**<br>**Snipped cilantro *or* parsley (optional)** | ● In a medium saucepan cook onion and garlic in butter or margarine till tender but not brown. Stir in corn-tomato mixture, remaining corn, broth, salt, pepper, and hot pepper sauce, if desired. Bring to boiling. Reduce heat and simmer for 20 to 25 minutes. Gradually stir in cream. Heat through, but *do not boil*. Season to taste. Garnish with cilantro or parsley, if desired. Makes 8 side-dish servings. |

**Using a sharp knife, cut the tips off the corn kernels. Hold ear of corn at an angle so one end rests in a small dish. Cut down across tips of the kernels toward the dish.**

**Holding the ear of corn at the same angle, scrape the ear with the knife, as shown. This two-step method of removing the kernels releases the milky liquid in the corn.**

# Pork and Hominy Soup

| | |
|---|---|
| **1 pound lean boneless pork, cut into ½-inch cubes**<br>**1 cup chopped onion**<br>**2 cloves garlic, minced**<br>**2 tablespoons cooking oil** | ● In a large saucepan or Dutch oven cook pork, onion, and garlic in hot oil till meat is brown and onion is tender. |
| **4 cups chicken broth**<br>**1½ teaspoons dried oregano, crushed**<br>**¼ teaspoon ground cumin**<br>**1 14½-ounce can hominy, drained**<br>**½ cup thinly sliced carrot**<br>**¼ cup chopped celery** | ● Stir in chicken broth, oregano, cumin, and ¼ teaspoon *pepper*. Bring to boiling. Reduce heat and simmer, covered, for 1 hour. Stir in hominy, carrot, and celery. Simmer, covered, for 30 minutes more. Skim off fat. |
| **Torn lettuce**<br>**Sliced radishes**<br>**Avocado slices**<br>**Salsa** | ● Top each serving with lettuce, radishes, avocado slices, and salsa. Makes 4 main-dish servings. |

**Originally this hearty soup was made from a pig's head, but using boneless pork is *much* easier!**

# Mexican Chicken Soup

*Pictured on pages 40–41.*

| | |
|---|---|
| 1 | 4½- to 5-pound stewing chicken, cut up |
| 6 | cups water |
| 3 | stalks celery, cut up |
| 1 | small onion, cut up |
| ¼ | teaspoon salt |
| ⅛ | teaspoon pepper |
| 1 | bay leaf |

● In a Dutch oven combine chicken pieces, water, celery, onion, salt, pepper, and bay leaf. Bring to boiling. Reduce heat and simmer, covered, for 2 hours or till chicken is tender. Remove chicken from broth. Let stand till chicken is cool enough to handle, then cut off meat and cube chicken. Set aside.

| | |
|---|---|
| 1 | 16-ounce can tomatoes, cut up |
| 3 | medium carrots, cut into julienne strips |
| ½ | cup chopped onion |
| 4 | teaspoons instant chicken bouillon granules |

● Meanwhile, strain broth, discarding vegetables and bay leaf. Skim off fat. Return broth to Dutch oven. Stir in *undrained* tomatoes, carrots, onion, and bouillon. Simmer, covered, for 20 minutes or till carrots are almost tender.

| | |
|---|---|
| 1 | small yellow summer squash *or* zucchini, halved lengthwise and sliced ¼ inch thick (about 1 cup) |
| 1 | small avocado, seeded, peeled, and sliced |

● Add chicken to broth mixture along with summer squash or zucchini. Simmer, covered, about 5 minutes more or till vegetables are tender.

Garnish each serving with avocado slices. Makes 8 main-dish servings.

U.S. cooks vie for blue ribbons with their pies and cinnamon rolls. But in Mexico, a cook's pride lies in making clear, delicate soup stocks like the one used in this soup.

Lime Soup

Tortilla Soup

# Lime Soup

| | | |
|---|---|---|
| 6 | cups chicken broth | ● In a large pan combine chicken broth and gizzards. Simmer, covered, 1 hour. |
| 4 | chicken gizzards | |

| | |
|---|---|
| 2 whole small chicken breasts (about 1¼ pounds total) | ● Add chicken breasts and simmer, covered, about 15 minutes. Add livers and simmer for 5 to 10 minutes more or till chicken breasts and livers are tender. Remove solids from broth. Let stand till cool enough to handle. Finely chop gizzards and livers. Skin, bone, and shred chicken breasts. Strain broth. |
| 4 chicken livers | |

| | |
|---|---|
| ½ cup chopped onion | ● Cook onion and garlic in hot oil till |
| 1 clove garlic, minced | tender but not brown. Add tomato, green |
| 1 tablespoon cooking oil | pepper, and oregano. Cook over |
| 1 large tomato, chopped | medium heat for 5 minutes. Remove |
| ⅓ cup chopped green pepper | from heat and stir into chicken broth. |
| ½ teaspoon dried oregano, crushed | Trim white membrane from peel. Stir peel and lime juice into broth mixture. |
| 4 1x½-inch slices grapefruit peel | Simmer, covered, for 30 minutes, then add chopped meat and shredded |
| 3 tablespoons lime juice | chicken. Heat through. Remove peel. |

| | |
|---|---|
| 6 Homemade Corn *or* Flour Tortillas (see recipes, pages 6–7) *or* purchased tortillas | ● Meanwhile, cut tortillas in half, then cut crosswise into ½-inch-wide strips. In a heavy skillet heat ½ inch oil. Fry strips in hot oil, about half at a time, for 40 to 45 seconds or till crisp and light brown. Drain on paper towels. |
| Cooking oil Thin lime slices Pickled serrano peppers, rinsed, seeded, and chopped Cracked black pepper | Divide fried tortilla strips among soup bowls. Ladle soup over strips and garnish with thin slices of lime. Serve with pickled peppers and cracked pepper. Makes 4 main-dish servings. |

*First,* the bad news: Lime Soup gets its distinctive flavor from a variety of limes grown only on the Yucatán Peninsula.

*Now,* the good news: We discovered you can duplicate the authentic flavor in this soup with *any* lime and a little bit of grapefruit peel.

Mexican Chicken Soup
*(see recipe, page 39)*

# Tortilla Soup

½ cup chopped onion
1 clove garlic, minced
1 tablespoon butter *or* margarine

● In a 3-quart saucepan cook onion and garlic in butter or margarine till tender but not brown.

Cilantro goes by a couple of aliases—coriander and Chinese parsley. The fresh leaf looks like a flattened parsley leaf, but has a stronger flavor and fragrance. Start out using cilantro sparingly till you find out how well you like it. Shop for it at Italian, Oriental, or Latin American food stores.

3½ cups chicken broth
1 14½-ounce can tomatoes, cut up
1 8-ounce can tomato sauce
1 4-ounce can green chili peppers, drained, seeded, and cut into strips
¼ cup snipped cilantro *or* parsley
1 teaspoon dried oregano, crushed

● Stir in chicken broth, *undrained* tomatoes, tomato sauce, chili peppers, cilantro or parsley, and oregano. Bring to boiling. Reduce heat and simmer, covered, for 20 minutes.

6 Homemade Corn *or* Flour Tortillas (see recipes, pages 6–7) *or* purchased tortillas
Cooking oil
1 cup shredded Monterey Jack cheese (4 ounces)

● Meanwhile, cut tortillas in half, then cut crosswise into ½-inch-wide strips. In a heavy skillet heat ½ inch oil. Fry strips in hot oil, about half at a time, for 40 to 45 seconds or till crisp and light brown. Drain on paper towels.

Divide fried tortilla strips and cheese among soup bowls. Ladle soup over strips and cheese. Serve immediately. Makes 6 to 8 side-dish servings.

# Garlic Soup

| | |
|---|---|
| 6 cloves garlic<br>1 tablespoon cooking oil<br>4 cups chicken broth<br>¼ teaspoon pepper | ● Crush garlic cloves using a garlic press or the flat side of a knife. In a medium saucepan cook garlic in hot oil for 1 to 2 minutes or till tender but not brown. Stir in chicken broth and pepper. Cover and simmer for 20 minutes. |
| 2 beaten eggs<br>½ cup onion and garlic croutons<br>Snipped cilantro *or* parsley (optional) | ● Pour beaten eggs slowly into hot soup in a thin stream, stirring gently till egg cooks and shreds finely.<br>    Serve immediately with croutons. Garnish with cilantro or parsley, if desired. Makes 4 side-dish servings. |

What do the Chinese and Mexicans have in common? Soup! The delicate texture of Garlic Soup may remind you of Chinese egg drop soup.

The key to making either soup is to stir the soup gently and keep it just simmering (not boiling) so that the eggs form fine threads rather than clumping into large pieces or turning the soup cloudy.

# Meatball Soup

| | |
|---|---|
| 1 beaten egg<br>⅓ cup soft bread crumbs<br>1 tablespoon snipped cilantro *or* parsley<br>1 tablespoon canned diced green chili peppers, drained<br>⅛ teaspoon salt<br>Dash pepper<br>¾ pound ground beef | ● For meatballs, in a medium mixing bowl stir together egg, bread crumbs, cilantro or parsley, chili peppers, salt, and pepper. Stir in ground beef and mix well. Shape mixture into 1-inch meatballs.<br>    Place meatballs in a large skillet. Cook over low heat for 15 to 20 minutes or till done. Drain off fat. |
| 2½ cups beef broth<br>⅓ cup tomato paste<br>1 small turnip, peeled and cubed (about ⅔ cup)<br>1 medium carrot, thinly sliced (about ½ cup)<br>¼ cup chopped onion<br>1 clove garlic, minced | ● Meanwhile, in a large saucepan combine broth and tomato paste. Bring to boiling, then add turnip, carrot, onion, and garlic. Reduce heat and simmer, covered, for 15 to 20 minutes. |
| 1 cup shredded cabbage | ● Stir meatballs and cabbage into soup. Cook 5 minutes more or till vegetables are tender. Makes 4 main-dish servings. |

Many a confused *turista* (tourist) has wandered out of a restaurant in Mexico pondering why he ended up with a plate of plain rice and not the bowl of rice soup he thought he had ordered! To keep it all straight, remember *sopa* indicates a soup like the ones in this chapter, while *sopa secas* (dry soups) are casserolelike dishes based on rice, tortillas, or pasta.

# Beef Stew In a Pot

| | |
|---|---|
| 1 **pound beef stew meat, cut into 1-inch cubes** | ● In a Dutch oven or large saucepan brown meat in hot oil. Stir in water, salt, and pepper. Cover and simmer 1 hour. |
| 1 **tablespoon cooking oil** | |
| 2 **cups water** | |
| ½ **teaspoon salt** | |
| **Dash pepper** | |

| | |
|---|---|
| 1 **dried ancho pepper** *and* 1 **dried pasilla pepper** *or* 1 **tablespoon chili powder** | ● Meanwhile, if using the dried peppers, cut them open and discard stems and seeds. Cut the peppers into small pieces with scissors or a knife. Place in a bowl and pour boiling water over the pepper pieces. Let stand 45 to 60 minutes or till pliable. Drain well. (See page 30.) |

| | |
|---|---|
| 1 **16-ounce can tomatoes** | ● In a blender container or food processor bowl place *undrained* tomatoes, onion, garlic, cumin, and drained peppers or chili powder. Cover and blend or process till nearly smooth. |
| 1 **medium onion, cut up** | |
| 1 **clove garlic** | |
| ⅛ **teaspoon ground cumin** | |

| | |
|---|---|
| 2 **medium potatoes, peeled and cut into 1-inch cubes** | ● Add tomato mixture to Dutch oven or saucepan along with potatoes and corn. Cover and simmer for 30 minutes. Stir in zucchini or summer squash. Cook for 5 to 10 minutes more or till meat is tender and vegetables are done. Makes 4 main-dish servings. |
| 1 **large fresh ear of corn, cut into 1-inch pieces** | |
| 1 **medium zucchini** *or* **yellow summer squash, halved lengthwise and sliced 1 inch thick** | |

This savory peasant soup owes its name to the decorated earthenware pot it's traditionally cooked in.

# Tablecloth-Stainer Stew

| | |
|---|---|
| 4 dried ancho peppers *and* 4 dried pasilla peppers *or* ¼ cup chili powder | ● If using the dried peppers, cut them open and discard stems and seeds. Cut peppers into small pieces with scissors or a knife. Place in a bowl and pour boiling water over pepper pieces. Let stand 45 to 60 minutes or till pliable. Drain well, reserving ⅓ cup water. (See page 30.) |
| 1 2½- to 3-pound broiler-fryer chicken, cut up<br>Salt<br>Pepper<br>2 tablespoons cooking oil *or* shortening<br>½ pound lean boneless pork, cut into 1-inch cubes | ● Meanwhile, rinse chicken, then pat dry. Season with salt and pepper. In a Dutch oven cook chicken pieces in hot oil or shortening, uncovered, over medium heat for 10 to 15 minutes or till light brown, turning to brown evenly. Remove chicken from Dutch oven and drain well, reserving drippings.<br>   Brown pork in drippings, then drain well and discard drippings. Return chicken and pork to Dutch oven. |
| 1 8-ounce can tomatoes<br>1 large onion, cut up<br>3 cloves garlic<br>1 teaspoon dried oregano<br>¼ teaspoon salt<br>¼ teaspoon ground cinnamon<br>¼ teaspoon pepper | ● In a blender container or food processor bowl combine *undrained* tomatoes, onion, garlic, oregano, salt, cinnamon, pepper, drained peppers or chili powder, and reserved water (if using chili powder, add ⅓ cup *water*). Cover and blend or process till smooth. |
| 3 cups chicken broth<br>1 medium jicama, peeled and cubed (about 1 cup)<br>1 ripe large plantain *or* 2 firm medium bananas, peeled and sliced<br>1 tart cooking apple, peeled, cored, and sliced<br>1 firm pear, peeled, cored, and sliced<br>1 8-ounce can pineapple chunks (juice pack), drained<br>2 tablespoons snipped cilantro *or* parsley | ● Stir tomato mixture and chicken broth into Dutch oven with chicken and pork. Bring to boiling over high heat. Stir in jicama and plantain (do not add bananas). Reduce heat and simmer, covered, over low heat for 45 minutes.<br>   Stir in apple and pear slices. Simmer, covered, for 5 minutes more. Stir in pineapple (if using bananas, add them now). Cover and heat through. Stir in cilantro or parsley. Makes 8 servings. |

**Better save your good linens for another time— this recipe didn't get its name for nothin'!**

Wrap marinated chicken in banana leaves that have been cut into about 12x9-inch rectangles.

# Chicken Baked In Banana Leaves

| | | |
|---|---|---|
| 1 teaspoon finely shredded orange peel<br>½ cup orange juice<br>2 teaspoons finely shredded lemon peel<br>¼ cup lemon juice<br>1 tablespoon chili powder<br>1 teaspoon whole black pepper<br>½ teaspoon dried oregano<br>½ teaspoon ground cumin<br>½ teaspoon ground allspice<br>¼ teaspoon salt<br>2 cloves garlic<br>1 cup chopped onion<br>1 2½- to 3-pound broiler-fryer chicken, cut up | ● For marinade, in a blender container or food processor bowl combine orange peel, orange juice, lemon peel, lemon juice, chili powder, pepper, oregano, cumin, allspice, salt, and garlic. Cover and blend or process till nearly smooth. Stir in onion.<br><br>Place chicken pieces in a large mixing bowl. Pour marinade over chicken. Marinate, covered, in refrigerator about 24 hours, turning pieces occasionally. | Try looking for banana leaves at ethnic food markets or check with your local florist. |
| Banana leaves (optional)<br>Foil | ● Cut banana leaves into six 12x9-inch rectangles. Divide chicken pieces among rectangles. Wrap banana leaves around each serving of chicken. Overwrap with foil and seal tightly. (If banana leaves are unavailable, just wrap chicken in foil rectangles and seal tightly.) | Mexican Rice: In a 10-inch skillet cook and stir ⅓ cup *uncooked long grain rice;* ¼ cup chopped *onion;* and 1 clove *garlic,* minced, over medium-high heat in 1 tablespoon *cooking oil* about 3 minutes or till rice is lightly browned. Stir in one *undrained* 16-ounce can *tomatoes,* cut up; ½ cup *chicken broth;* ½ teaspoon dried *oregano,* crushed; and ⅛ teaspoon *pepper.* Bring to boiling. Reduce heat and simmer, covered, for 15 minutes. Stir in 1 cup frozen *peas.* Cook about 5 minutes more or till rice is done and liquid is absorbed. Stir in ⅓ cup chopped red or green *sweet pepper.* Makes 6 servings. |
| Mexican Rice (see recipe, right) (optional) | ● Place wrapped chicken pieces in a single layer in a shallow baking pan. Bake in a 375° oven about 50 minutes or till tender. Remove foil. Serve chicken in banana leaves with Mexican Rice, if desired. Makes 6 servings. | |

**Wrap foil around each banana leaf bundle and seal tightly.**

**Serve chicken in banana leaves with Mexican Rice.**

# Chicken with Mole Sauce

|  |  |
|---|---|
| 2 dried ancho, mulato, *or* pasilla peppers *or* a combination of two varieties | ● Cut peppers open and discard stems and seeds. Cut the peppers into small pieces with scissors or a knife. Place in a bowl and pour boiling water over the pepper pieces. Let stand 45 to 60 minutes or till pliable. Drain well. (See page 30.) |
| 1 2½- to 3-pound broiler-fryer chicken, cut up<br>Salt<br>Pepper<br>2 tablespoons cooking oil *or* shortening | ● Meanwhile, rinse chicken, then pat dry. Season with salt and pepper. In a large skillet or Dutch oven cook chicken pieces in hot oil or shortening, uncovered, over medium heat for 10 to 15 minutes or till light brown, turning to brown evenly. Remove chicken from skillet or Dutch oven and set aside. Drain skillet or Dutch oven. |
| ¾ cup chicken broth<br>1 medium tomato, peeled and cut up<br>¼ cup slivered almonds<br>¼ cup chopped onion<br>1 to 2 canned jalapeño peppers<br>2 tablespoons raisins<br>1 tablespoon sesame seed<br>2 cloves garlic<br>1 teaspoon sugar<br>½ teaspoon salt<br>⅛ teaspoon aniseed<br>⅛ teaspoon ground cinnamon<br>⅛ teaspoon ground coriander<br>⅛ teaspoon ground nutmeg<br>½ square (½ ounce) unsweetened chocolate | ● For mole sauce, in a blender container or food processor bowl combine chicken broth, tomato, almonds, onion, jalapeño peppers, raisins, sesame seed, garlic, sugar, salt, aniseed, cinnamon, coriander, nutmeg, and drained peppers. Cover and blend or process to a coarse puree. Transfer sauce mixture to skillet or Dutch oven and add chocolate. Cook and stir over low heat to combine ingredients and melt chocolate. |
| Hot cooked rice<br>2 tablespoons toasted slivered almonds | ● Add chicken to sauce mixture in skillet or Dutch oven. Cover and simmer for 25 to 30 minutes or till chicken is tender, turning once.<br>    To serve, transfer chicken to a serving platter with rice. Skim fat from sauce. Pour sauce over chicken and rice. Sprinkle with almonds. Makes 6 servings. |

Moles (MOH-lays) and chocolate go together hand in glove. But a true mole isn't really a chocolate sauce. Only one small piece of chocolate goes into a large pot full of this dark-brown chili pepper concoction.

The specific dried pepper or combination of peppers you use (*not* the chocolate) determine the flavor of the mole sauce. The ancho is the most widely used pepper in Mexican cooking and gives moles a mild to medium hotness. The mulato pepper gives a slightly sweeter mole, but is harder to find. Pasilla peppers produce a more piquant mole that's slightly hotter than the ancho version.

# Pork and Peppers

| | |
|---|---|
| 2 **pounds lean boneless pork, cut into 1-inch cubes** | ● In a large saucepan brown *half* of the pork in hot oil. With a slotted spoon, remove pork. Set aside. Add the remaining pork, onion, garlic, and cumin. Cook till meat is brown. Return all the pork to the saucepan. |
| 2 **tablespoons cooking oil** | |
| 1 **large onion, thinly sliced and separated into rings** | |
| 2 **cloves garlic, minced** | |
| 1 **teaspoon ground cumin** | |

*Tomatillos* (toh-mah-TEE-yohs) are small, olive-green fruit covered with brown, thin, papery husks that you pull off before using. When buying fresh tomatillos, avoid the shriveled or bruised ones. To store them, refrigerate, unwashed, between paper towels for up to 4 weeks. Look for canned tomatillos in Latin American sections of larger supermarkets.

| | |
|---|---|
| 3 *or* 4 **large Anaheim peppers,** *or* **two 4-ounce cans diced green chili peppers, drained** | ● If using fresh peppers, loosen skins by broiling peppers 4 inches from heat till charred on all sides, turning once. Place the charred peppers in a paper bag. Close the bag tightly and let stand 10 minutes. Remove peppers from bag. Peel skin away from flesh and cut off stems. Slit peppers open and scrape away seeds and ribs; coarsely chop. (See page 30.) |
| 5 *or* 6 **fresh tomatillos, chopped,** *or* **one 13-ounce can tomatillos, drained, rinsed, and cut up** | |
| 1 **cup chicken broth** | Stir tomatillos, broth, peppers, tomato, and oregano into saucepan. Bring to boiling. Reduce heat and simmer, covered, about 1½ hours or till meat is tender. Uncover and boil gently for 20 to 30 minutes more or till slightly thickened, stirring occasionally. Stir in lime juice. |
| 1 **large tomato, chopped** | |
| 1 **teaspoon dried oregano, crushed** | |
| 2 **teaspoons lime juice** | |

| | |
|---|---|
| **Hot cooked rice** | ● To serve, spoon pork mixture over rice and sprinkle with toasted almonds. Makes 6 servings. |
| 2 **tablespoons toasted slivered almonds** | |

# Chicken with Pumpkin Seed Sauce

| | |
|---|---|
| 2 **whole large chicken breasts (about 2½ pounds total), skinned, boned, and halved lengthwise** | ● Roll chicken breasts in flour to coat. Dip in egg, then coat with bread crumbs. Heat butter or margarine in a medium skillet. Add chicken breasts and cook over low heat, uncovered, for 25 to 30 minutes or till chicken is tender, turning to brown evenly. Drain on paper towels. |
| 3 **tablespoons all-purpose flour** | |
| 1 **beaten egg** | |
| ½ **cup fine dry bread crumbs** | |
| 2 **tablespoons butter** *or* **margarine** | |

**Pumpkin Seed Sauce:** In a blender container or food processor bowl combine one 13-ounce can *tomatillos,* drained and rinsed; 3 tablespoons *pumpkin seed;* 2 tablespoons sliced *almonds;* 1 tablespoon snipped *cilantro or parsley;* and 1 *jalapeño pepper,* seeded and coarsely chopped. Cover and blend or process to a coarse puree. Transfer to a saucepan. Heat through. Makes about 1 cup.

| | |
|---|---|
| **Pumpkin Seed Sauce (see recipe, right)** | ● To serve, arrange chicken breasts on a serving platter. Spoon Pumpkin Seed Sauce over chicken. Garnish with cilantro or parsley, if desired. Makes 4 servings. |
| **Snipped cilantro** *or* **parsley (optional)** | |

# One-Pot Spanish Ribs

8 ounces pork sausage links
1 cup chopped onion
1 clove garlic, minced
2½ pounds pork loin back ribs, cut into 6 serving-size portions

● Cut sausage links in half. In a large saucepan or Dutch oven cook the sausage pieces, onion, and garlic till sausage is brown and onion is tender. Remove from pan and drain. Brown the ribs, half at a time, in same pan. Return sausage mixture and all ribs to pan.

Sop up every last drop of the thick and rich gravy with chewy rolls, like the Bolillos on page 92.

1 28-ounce can tomatoes, cut up
2 tablespoons chopped canned jalapeño peppers
2 teaspoons dried oregano, crushed
2 medium zucchini, cut into ½-inch-thick slices (about 3 cups)
1 large red *or* green sweet pepper, cut into bite-size pieces

● Stir in *undrained* tomatoes, jalapeño peppers, and oregano. Simmer, covered, for 50 minutes or till ribs are tender. Add zucchini and sweet pepper. Simmer, covered, for 10 to 15 minutes more or till vegetables are tender.
  Use a slotted spoon to transfer ribs, sausage, and vegetables to a serving platter. Keep warm.

⅓ cup cold water
3 tablespoons all-purpose flour
½ cup sliced pitted ripe olives

● For gravy, skim fat from pan juices, then measure juices. Add enough water, if necessary, to make 2 cups liquid. Return juices to pan. Combine water and flour, then stir into pan juices. Cook and stir till thickened and bubbly. Stir in olives, then cook and stir 1 minute more.

½ cup shredded cheddar cheese (2 ounces)

● Spoon some of the gravy over meat and vegetables on platter. Sprinkle with cheese. Pass remaining gravy. Serves 6.

| 3 | dried ancho peppers *or* 3 tablespoons chili powder | ● If using the dried peppers, cut them open and discard stems and seeds. Cut the peppers into small pieces with scissors or a knife. Place in a bowl and pour boiling water over the pepper pieces. Let stand 45 to 60 minutes or till pliable. Drain well. (See page 30.) | **Adobo,** a concentrated paste of ground chilies, spices, herbs, and vinegar, was originally used for pickling meat. In this recipe, we diluted the adobo with a little tomato sauce to make a flavor-filled sauce. |

| | | |
|---|---|---|
| 1 | medium onion, cut up | ● For adobo sauce, in a blender container or food processor bowl place onion, tomato sauce, vinegar, flour, oregano, cumin seed, garlic, drained peppers or chili powder, and ¼ teaspoon *salt*. Cover and blend or process till nearly smooth. |
| ½ | cup tomato sauce | |
| 2 | tablespoons vinegar | |
| 1 | tablespoon all-purpose flour | |
| ½ | teaspoon dried oregano | |
| ¼ | teaspoon cumin seed | Pour sauce into a 10-inch skillet. Place chops in sauce, turning once to coat both sides. Simmer chops, covered, over low heat about 45 minutes or till tender. |
| 2 | cloves garlic | |
| 4 | pork loin chops, cut ½ inch thick and trimmed of excess fat | |

| | | |
|---|---|---|
| | Lettuce leaves<br>Dairy sour cream<br>Radish roses *or* sliced radishes<br>Sliced avocado | ● Arrange chops on a lettuce-lined serving platter. Spoon sauce over chops. Dollop with sour cream and garnish with radishes and avocado. Makes 4 servings. |

# Stuffed Peppers with Walnut Topper

| | |
|---|---|
| 6 large poblano peppers *or* green peppers<br>Salt | ● If using poblano peppers, cut a lengthwise slit in 1 side of each pepper. Carefully remove seeds and veins, leaving stems intact. (If using green peppers, cut off tops and carefully remove seeds and veins.) Cook peppers in a large amount of boiling water about 5 minutes or till crisp-tender. Drain well. Sprinkle insides of peppers with salt. |
| Picadillo (see recipe, page 14)<br>Walnut Topper<br>¼ cup pomegranate seeds (optional) | ● Spoon Picadillo into peppers. Place in a 12x7½x2-inch baking dish. Bake, covered, in a 350° oven for 25 to 30 minutes or till heated through.<br><br>Halve peppers before serving, if desired. Serve with Walnut Topper. Sprinkle with pomegranate seeds, if desired. Makes 6 servings. |

**Walnut Topper:** In a blender container or food processor bowl combine ½ cup *walnuts;* one 3-ounce package *cream cheese,* softened; ⅓ cup *milk;* and ¼ teaspoon ground *cinnamon.* Cover and blend or process till smooth. Chill thoroughly. Makes about 1 cup.

When the Treaty of Cordoba was signed in 1821, it marked the beginning of Mexican independence from Spain. To celebrate, the people of Puebla (now a Mexican state) concocted many dishes whose ingredients matched the colors of the Mexican flag—green, white, and red.

This dish, now one of the most famous in all Mexico, uses green poblano peppers, white walnut-cream-cheese sauce, and red pomegranate seeds.

# Name That Food

So you think your Spanish is pretty good, huh? Well, try this little mix and match food game. Match the Mexican recipe title on the left with the translated title on the right. The answers are at the bottom.

| | |
|---|---|
| 1. Huevos Rancheros | A. Rich Cooked Eggnog |
| 2. Ceviche | B. Ranch-Style Eggs |
| 3. Chiles Rellenos | C. Sweet Rolls |
| 4. Nachos | D. Stuffed Chilies |
| 5. Pozole | E. Crusty Rolls |
| 6. Guacamole | F. Dessert Turnovers |
| 7. Flan | G. Avocado Sauce |
| 8. Quesadillas | H. Caramel Custard |
| 9. Picadillo | I. Fried Biscuit Puffs |
| 10. Bolillos | J. Pork and Hominy Soup |
| 11. Sangria | K. Mexican Hash |
| 12. Rompope | L. Red Wine Punch |
| 13. Pan Dulce | M. Marinated Seafood |
| 14. Café de Olla | N. Cheese Turnovers |
| 15. Sopaipillas | O. Cheese and Chili Chips |
| 16. Empanadas | P. Pot Coffee |

1.B; 2.M; 3.D; 4.O; 5.J; 6.G; 7.H; 8.N; 9.K; 10.E; 11.L; 12.A; 13.C; 14.P; 15.I; 16.F

# Texas Bowls of Red

20 dried hot peppers *or*
    2 tablespoons crushed
    red pepper
2 dried ancho peppers *or* 2
    tablespoons chili
    powder

● Crush hot chili peppers. Remove stems and seeds from ancho peppers, then cut into 1-inch pieces. Put all peppers into a blender container or food processor bowl. Cover and blend or process till ground. *Let pepper dust settle before opening blender or food processor.* (See page 30.) (If using crushed red pepper and chili powder, stir them together.)

3 slices bacon
2½ pounds beef round steak,
    cut into ½-inch cubes
1 cup chopped onion
2 cloves garlic, minced
1 teaspoon ground cumin

● In a large saucepan cook bacon till crisp. Drain, reserving 2 tablespoons drippings in saucepan. Crumble bacon and set aside.
    Brown *half* the beef in reserved drippings. Remove meat and set aside. Add remaining meat, onion, garlic, cumin, and pepper mixture. Cook till meat is brown. Return all meat to pan.

1 12-ounce can beer
1 10½-ounce can
    condensed beef broth
1 teaspoon dried oregano,
    crushed
    Hot cooked rice
    Hot cooked pinto beans

● Stir in beer, beef broth, oregano, crumbled bacon, and ¼ teaspoon *pepper.* Bring to boiling. Reduce heat and simmer, uncovered, for 1 to 1¼ hours or till meat is tender, stirring occasionally. Serve with hot cooked rice and beans. Makes 6 to 8 servings.

*Nothing* in Texas—not politics, not religion, not even taxes—can spark an argument faster than a discussion about chili. To Texans, there are two unbreakable rules for authentic "Texas-style" chili. Use cubed beef, not ground beef. And *never* add beans to the meat mixture—serve them alongside or not at all.

# Northerners' Chili

1 pound ground beef
1 cup chopped onion
1 clove garlic, minced

● In a large saucepan cook beef, onion, and garlic till meat is brown and onion is tender. Drain off fat.

1 16-ounce can tomatoes,
    cut up
1 15½-ounce can red kidney
    beans, drained
½ cup orange juice
½ cup tequila, beer, *or* water
½ of a 6-ounce can (⅓ cup)
    tomato paste
1 4-ounce can diced green
    chili peppers, drained
½ teaspoon ground cumin
¼ teaspoon ground cloves
    Dairy sour cream
    Chopped avocado
    Shredded cheddar cheese
    Chopped tomato

● Stir in *undrained* tomatoes; kidney beans; orange juice; tequila, beer, or water; tomato paste; chili peppers; cumin; cloves; and ¼ teaspoon *salt.* Bring to boiling. Reduce heat and simmer, covered, for 30 minutes.
    Serve chili with sour cream, avocado, cheese, and tomato. Serves 4 to 6.

To folks up north, this mild chili with ground beef, tomatoes, and beans is "real" chili.

# Drunken Fish

2 1¼- to 1½-pound *or* one
   2½- to 3-pound fresh
   *or* frozen dressed red
   snapper (with tail)*
2 dried ancho peppers *or* 2
   tablespoons chili
   powder
⅓ cup dry red wine

● Thaw fish, if frozen. Meanwhile, if using the dried peppers, cut them open and discard stems and seeds. Cut the peppers into small pieces with scissors or a knife. Place in a bowl and pour boiling water over the pepper pieces. Let stand 45 to 60 minutes or till pliable. Drain well. (See page 30.)

   Combine wine and drained peppers or chili powder in a blender container or food processor bowl. Cover and blend or process till nearly smooth.

**To serve a cooked fish, use the tip of a sharp knife to cut a ½-inch-deep slit along the back, as shown above. Cut the upper fillet into serving-size pieces (see full-page photo, left). Slide a spatula under each piece along the backbone and transfer to a serving plate. Remove the skin.**

½ cup chopped onion
1 clove garlic, minced
1 tablespoon cooking oil
1 16-ounce can tomatoes,
   cut up
¼ cup snipped parsley
1 teaspoon sugar
½ teaspoon dried oregano,
   crushed
¼ teaspoon salt
¼ teaspoon ground cumin

● For sauce, in a medium saucepan cook onion and garlic in hot oil till tender but not brown. Stir in *undrained* tomatoes, parsley, sugar, oregano, salt, cumin, and wine mixture. Bring mixture to boiling. Reduce heat and simmer, covered, for 5 minutes.

Salt
Pepper
½ cup sliced pimiento-
   stuffed olives
1 tablespoon capers,
   drained (optional)
Parsley
Lemon slices
Hot cooked rice (optional)

● Place fish in a greased 13x9x2-inch baking dish. Season cavity with salt and pepper. Stir olives and capers, if desired, into sauce, then pour sauce over fish.

   Bake, covered, in a 350° oven till fish flakes easily when tested with a fork (allow 6 to 9 minutes for every ½ pound of fish). Carefully transfer fish to a serving platter. Garnish with parsley and lemon slices. Serve with rice, if desired. Pass sauce. Makes 4 servings.

**Note:** If you like, substitute 1½ pounds fresh or individually frozen *red snapper fillets* for the dressed fish. Bake, uncovered, in a 350° oven for 18 to 20 minutes or till fish flakes easily when tested with a fork.

**When the entire upper fillet has been removed, carefully pull the thick backbone free from the lower fillet. Cut the lower fillet into serving-size pieces and serve.**

# Snapper Veracruz

| | | |
|---|---|---|
| 1 pound fresh *or* frozen red snapper fillets *or* other fish fillets<br>3 medium potatoes (1 pound) | ● Thaw fish, if frozen. Scrub potatoes, then peel and quarter each one. Cook potatoes, covered, in boiling salted water for 20 to 25 minutes or till tender. Drain and keep warm. | **There are as many versions of this colorful dish as there are red snappers swimming in the Gulf of Mexico! Even so, no matter what recipe you use, the traditonal tomato-base sauce should always be full of garlic, onion, peppers, and a hint of cinnamon. And don't forget the potatoes—they help cut the hotness from the peppers.** |
| ¼ cup all-purpose flour<br>⅛ teaspoon salt<br>⅛ teaspoon pepper<br>1 tablespoon cooking oil | ● Meanwhile, in a small mixing bowl stir together flour, salt, and pepper. Coat fish fillets on both sides with flour mixture.<br><br>In a 10-inch skillet cook fillets in hot oil over medium heat for 4 to 5 minutes on each side or till fish flakes easily when tested with a fork. Remove fish from skillet and keep warm. | |
| 1 large onion, sliced and separated into rings<br>2 cloves garlic, minced<br>1 tablespoon cooking oil | ● For sauce, in the skillet cook onion and garlic in hot cooking oil till onion is tender but not brown. | **If you purchase Pacific snapper (also called rockfish) rather than red snapper, fry the fillets a minute or so longer to compensate for the extra thickness of the fillets.** |
| 1 16-ounce can tomatoes, cut up<br>¼ cup sliced pimiento-stuffed olives<br>¼ cup dry white wine<br>2 tablespoons capers, drained<br>2 teaspoons seeded and chopped canned jalapeño pepper<br>½ teaspoon sugar<br>1 bay leaf<br>Several dashes ground cinnamon | ● Stir in *undrained* tomatoes, olives, wine, capers, jalapeño pepper, sugar, bay leaf, and cinnamon. Bring sauce mixture to boiling. Boil gently, uncovered, for 5 to 7 minutes or till mixture is slightly thickened. Add cooked fish fillets to sauce. Heat through. Remove bay leaf. | |
| Snipped cilantro *or* parsley (optional) | ● Arrange fish and potatoes on a serving platter. Spoon sauce atop. Garnish with cilantro or parsley, if desired. Makes 4 servings. | |

# Baked Chiles Rellenos ✓

| | |
|---|---|
| 3 large poblano peppers *or* green peppers | ● Halve peppers lengthwise and carefully remove stems, seeds, and veins. |
| 6 ounces Monterey Jack, cheddar, havarti, *or* mozzarella cheese | ● Fill each pepper half with cheese, cutting cheese into pieces to fit. Place filled pepper halves, cut side up, in a well-greased 10x6x2-inch baking dish. |
| 4 beaten eggs<br>⅓ cup milk<br>½ cup all-purpose flour<br>½ teaspoon baking powder<br>¼ teaspoon salt<br>1 cup shredded Monterey Jack, cheddar, havarti, *or* mozzarella cheese (4 ounces) | ● In a medium mixing bowl combine eggs and milk. Add flour, baking powder, and salt. Beat with a rotary beater till smooth. Pour egg mixture over peppers. Bake, uncovered, in a 450° oven for 15 minutes. Sprinkle with shredded cheese. |
| Red Chili Sauce (see recipe, page 35) *or* Green Chili Sauce (see recipe, page 35)<br>Dairy sour cream | ● Serve peppers with warm Red Chili Sauce or Green Chili Sauce and top with sour cream. Makes 6 main-dish servings. |

We're *always* on the lookout for ways to streamline recipes and shorten the time you spend in the kitchen. This casserole version of the classic Chiles Rellenos (CHEE-lehs reh-YEH-nohs) is a good example. Rather than wrestle with the traditional method of dipping the stuffed chilies in batter and frying, we placed the stuffed chilies in a baking dish and poured the batter over the top—less work *and* less mess, but just as delicious.

# Huevos Rancheros

| | |
|---|---|
| 2 tablespoons cooking oil<br>4 6-inch Corn Tortillas (see recipe, page 6), 8-inch Flour Tortillas (see recipe, page 7), *or* purchased tortillas<br>8 eggs<br>1 tablespoon water | ● In a heavy 12-inch skillet heat cooking oil. Fry each tortilla in hot oil for 10 seconds or till limp. Drain on paper towels. Keep tortillas warm in a 300° oven while preparing eggs.<br>  In same skillet reheat cooking oil. Carefully break eggs into skillet. When whites are set and edges cooked, add water. Cover skillet and cook eggs to desired doneness. |
| Ranchero Salsa (see recipe, page 34) *or* Green Chili Sauce (see recipe, page 35)<br>½ cup shredded Monterey Jack cheese (2 ounces)<br>Avocado slices<br>Cilantro *or* parsley sprigs | ● Place tortillas on 4 dinner plates. Top *each* with *2* fried eggs. Spoon some warm Ranchero Salsa or Green Chili Sauce over each. Sprinkle with cheese. Garnish with avocado slices and cilantro or parsley. Serve immediately. Makes 4 servings. |

When you hear Huevos Rancheros (WEH-vohs rahn-CHEH-rohs) don't automatically think breakfast. Instead, serve it with refried beans and a tossed salad for a great lunch or supper.

# Make Mine Vanilla

For centuries, the Aztec Indians used vanilla beans for medicine, money, and perfume. Thank goodness those days are gone so that today we have lots of vanilla for cooking. You'll find vanilla in three forms at the grocery store—pure extract, imitation flavoring, and whole beans. Although the flavoring is a bit weaker, it and the extract are interchangeable. And what can you use the whole beans for? They're great for spicing up homemade liqueurs and flavored coffees. Or, try making your own vanilla sugar by splitting a couple of beans in half and putting them in a canister of sugar. Let the sugar stand about 2 weeks, then use this delicate treat in homemade cakes and cookies.

# Flan

½ cup sugar

● To caramelize the sugar, in a small heavy skillet heat sugar over medium heat, stirring constantly, for 8 to 10 minutes or till sugar melts and turns a rich brown color (see top photo, right).

Remove skillet from heat and immediately pour caramelized sugar into a 4½-cup metal ring mold (8-inch diameter). Holding mold with potholders, quickly rotate mold so sugar coats the bottom and sides evenly (see bottom photo, right).

For more of that great vanilla flavor, use some of your own vanilla sugar (see tip, opposite).

6 eggs
3 cups milk
½ cup sugar
1½ teaspoons vanilla
1 teaspoon grated orange peel

● In a large mixing bowl lightly beat eggs. Stir in milk, sugar, vanilla, and orange peel. Place caramel-coated ring mold in a 9x9x2-inch or 13x9x2-inch baking pan on an oven rack. Pour egg mixture into mold.

Pour the *hottest* tap water available into the baking pan around the mold to a depth of 1 inch. Bake in a 325° oven for 50 to 53 minutes or till a knife inserted halfway between center and edge comes out clean. Remove the mold from the hot water. Cool flan on a wire rack. Chill for at least 3½ hours.

**Caramelizing sugar actually means heating and melting it till it turns a golden brown.**

Place the sugar in a heavy skillet and cook it over medium heat, stirring with a wooden spatula or spoon, till the sugar melts and turns a rich brown color. Be sure to stir constantly so the sugar doesn't scorch.

Sliced strawberries
Peeled and sliced kiwi fruit
Strawberry halves (optional)

● To unmold flan, loosen edges with a spatula. Slip end of spatula down sides to let air in. Invert mold onto a serving platter. Spoon any caramel mixture that remains in mold atop custard. Pile sliced fruit into center. Garnish flan with strawberry halves, if desired. Makes 10 to 12 servings.

**Pour the hot sugar into the metal ring mold and quickly rotate it so the sugar coats the bottom and sides evenly. The mold will get *very* hot, so be sure to use potholders.**

# Flaming Plantains

| | |
|---|---|
| 3 ripe medium plantains *or* 6 firm medium bananas<br>Lemon juice | ● Peel plantains or bananas and bias slice (you should have about 3 cups). Toss with lemon juice |
| ¼ cup butter *or* margarine<br>⅓ cup packed brown sugar<br>⅓ cup orange juice<br>1 tablespoon lime juice | ● For sauce, melt butter or margarine in a 10-inch skillet. Stir in brown sugar, orange juice, and lime juice. Cook, uncovered, over medium heat for 4 to 5 minutes or till sauce is thick and syrupy, stirring frequently. |
| 3 tablespoons coffee liqueur | ● Add plantains to sauce. Cook and stir gently for 5 to 7 minutes or till tender. (If using bananas, cook and stir just till heated through.) Gently stir in liqueur. Transfer mixture to a serving container. |
| 3 tablespoons rum<br>Vanilla ice cream | ● Heat rum in a small skillet or saucepan over low heat just till hot. Remove from heat. Carefully ignite rum and pour over plantains. Serve immediately over ice cream. Serves 6. |

**The first time you see a plantain, you might think it's just an overgrown banana. But besides being longer and bigger around than bananas, plantains are also less sweet and need to be cooked before you eat them. Bring them home from the super-market and, before you use them, let them ripen till the skins are totally black and the fruit is soft.**

# Mexican Wedding Cookies

| | |
|---|---|
| 1 cup butter *or* margarine<br>½ cup sifted powdered sugar<br>2 teaspoons water<br>1 teaspoon vanilla<br>2 cups all-purpose flour<br>½ cup ground toasted almonds *or* pecans<br>¼ teaspoon ground cinnamon *or* ½ teaspoon finely shredded orange, lemon, *or* tangerine peel<br>Powdered sugar | ● In a large mixer bowl beat butter or margarine till softened. Add powdered sugar and beat till fluffy. Add water and vanilla and beat well. Stir in flour, nuts, and cinnamon or orange, lemon, or tangerine peel.<br><br>Shape dough into 1-inch balls. Flatten slightly with the bottom of a glass dipped in powdered sugar. (If necessary, chill dough till easy to handle.) Place on an ungreased cookie sheet. |
| | ● Bake in a 325° oven for 18 to 20 minutes or till lightly browned on the bottom. Cool on cookie sheet for 5 minutes, then remove and roll cookies in powdered sugar. Cool thoroughly on wire racks. In a plastic bag, gently shake a few cookies at a time in powdered sugar. Makes about 55 cookies. |

**Our friends south of the Rio Grande like to wrap these shortbread cookies individually in white tissue paper. Then they twist and shred the ends of the tissue paper so the cookies look like bonbons.**

# Dessert Empanadas

| | |
|---|---|
| **2** cups all-purpose flour<br>**½** teaspoon salt<br>**⅔** cup shortening *or* lard<br>**6** to 7 tablespoons cold<br>water | ● For pastry, in a medium mixing bowl stir together flour and salt. Cut in the shortening or lard till pieces are the size of small peas. Sprinkle *1 tablespoon* of the water over part of the mixture, then gently toss with a fork. Push to side of bowl. Repeat till all is moistened. Form dough into a ball. |
| | ● On a lightly floured surface, roll *half* of the dough out to slightly less than ⅛-inch thickness. Cut into four 5½-inch circles. Repeat with remaining dough. |
| **Cinnamon-Apricot Filling,<br>Pumpkin Filling,** *or*<br>**Almond Filling**<br>**Milk**<br>**Sugar** | ● Spoon about ⅛ of the desired filling onto center of *each* circle. Moisten edges with water and fold in half, sealing edges with tines of a fork.<br>    Place turnovers on an ungreased baking sheet. Brush with milk, then sprinkle with sugar. Bake in a 375° oven for 20 to 25 minutes or till bottoms are lightly browned. Serve warm or cold. Makes 8 turnovers. |
| | **Cinnamon-Apricot Filling:** Put 8 ounces *dried apricots* (about 2½ cups) in a medium saucepan. Add enough water to cover. Bring to boiling. Reduce heat and simmer, covered, for 20 minutes. Drain. In a blender container or food processor bowl combine 1 cup *sugar,* 1 teaspoon ground *cinnamon,* ½ teaspoon ground *nutmeg,* and drained apricots. Cover and blend or process till almost smooth, stopping machine occasionally to scrape down sides. |
| | **Pumpkin Filling:** In a small mixing bowl stir together ½ of a 16-ounce can (about 1 cup) *pumpkin,* ⅓ cup packed *brown sugar,* ½ teaspoon ground *cinnamon,* and a dash ground *cloves.* Stir in ½ cup chopped *walnuts.* |
| | **Almond Filling:** In a small mixer bowl beat together one 8-ounce package *cream cheese,* softened; ½ cup sifted *powdered sugar;* 2 tablespoons *milk;* and ½ teaspoon *almond extract.* Stir in ½ cup chopped toasted *almonds.* |

Anything is fair game when it comes to filling these Mexican turnovers. Dessert turnovers like these can be filled with fruit, cheese, and nut combinations, or pumpkin and sweet potato mixtures.

Common savory fillings include seafood, chicken or turkey with leftover mole sauce, and Picadillo, (see recipe, page 14).

# Fried Ice Cream

| | |
|---|---|
| **1 pint ice cream** | ● Place 4 scoops (about ½ cup each) of ice cream in a small pan. Freeze for 1 hour or till firm. |
| **1 beaten egg**<br>**¼ teaspoon vanilla**<br>**2½ cups sweetened corn flakes, crushed**<br>**½ teaspoon ground cinnamon** | ● In a small mixing bowl stir together egg and vanilla. In a pie plate carefully stir together cereal and cinnamon.<br>    Dip each frozen ice-cream ball in the egg mixture, then roll it in cereal mixture. Return coated ice-cream balls to pan and freeze for 1 hour or till firm. Reserve remaining cereal mixture. |
| **1 beaten egg**<br>**¼ teaspoon vanilla** | ● In a small mixing bowl stir together egg and vanilla. Remove coated ice-cream balls from the freezer. Dip balls in egg mixture, then roll them in remaining cereal mixture. Return to pan. Cover and freeze for several hours or till firm. |
| **Cooking oil for deep-fat frying**<br>**Whipped cream (optional)**<br>**Mint sprigs (optional)** | ● In a deep-fat fryer or heavy saucepan fry frozen, coated ice-cream balls, 1 or 2 at a time, in deep hot oil (375°) for 15 seconds or till golden brown. Drain on paper towels. Return the fried ice-cream balls to the freezer while frying the remaining balls. Serve immediately with whipped cream and garnish with mint, if desired. Makes 4 servings. |

Dip the frozen ice-cream balls in the egg mixture, then roll them in the cereal mixture. Make sure the cereal completely covers the ice cream.

Place the four coated ice-cream balls in a small pan (or on a baking sheet) and put them into the freezer till they're firm.

Fry the ice-cream balls in hot oil about 15 seconds or till golden. Drain well on paper towels. Serve the fried ice-cream balls immediately with whipped cream and a mint sprig, or try them with jam or ice-cream topping.

# Chocolate-Cinnamon Ice Cream

2 cups sugar
2 envelopes unflavored gelatin
4 cups light cream
3 squares (3 ounces) semisweet chocolate, cut up
1 square (1 ounce) unsweetened chocolate, cut up
½ teaspoon ground cinnamon

● In a large saucepan combine sugar and gelatin. Stir in cream, cut-up chocolate, and ground cinnamon.
   Cook and stir over medium heat till mixture almost boils, stirring constantly to dissolve sugar and melt chocolate.

2 beaten eggs

● Stir about *1 cup* of the hot mixture into beaten eggs, then return all to saucepan. Cook and stir over low heat for 2 minutes. (If chocolate flecks appear, beat till smooth.) Cover and chill.

4 cups whipping cream
½ teaspoon vanilla
   Coffee liqueur
   Fried Cinnamon Chips (see recipe, right) (optional)

● Stir in cream and vanilla. Freeze in a 4- or 5-quart ice cream freezer according to manufacturer's directions.
   Top each serving with coffee liqueur. Serve with Fried Cinnamon Chips, if desired. Makes about 2½ quarts.

**Fried Cinnamon Chips:** In a shallow mixing bowl combine ½ cup *sugar* and ¾ teaspoon ground *cinnamon*. Set aside.
   In a heavy 10-inch skillet heat about 1 inch *cooking oil* to 360°. Meanwhile, cut 8 *flour tortillas* into quarters.
   Fry tortilla quarters, 3 or 4 at a time, about 1 minute on each side or till crisp and brown. Drain on paper towels. Coat chips with sugar-cinnamon mixture while warm. Makes 32.

# Tequila Sunrise Slush

½ cup water
⅓ cup sugar
1½ cups unsweetened pink grapefruit juice
¼ cup tequila
1 tablespoon grenadine syrup

● In a small saucepan bring water to boiling. Add sugar, stirring till dissolved. Remove from heat and stir in grapefruit juice, tequila, and grenadine.
   Pour mixture into a 9x9x2-inch baking pan. Cover and freeze about 2 hours or till nearly firm. Break frozen mixture into chunks and transfer to a chilled small mixer bowl. Beat with an electric mixer on low speed till fluffy. Cover and freeze till serving time, stirring once or twice.

1 tablespoon sugar
¼ teaspoon ground nutmeg

● In a shallow dish stir together sugar and nutmeg. To serve, rub the rim of sherbet dishes or glasses with a little water. Invert glasses into dish with sugar-nutmeg mixture. Spoon slush mixture into prepared dishes. Makes 4 servings.

Put out the fire from a hot and spicy meal like Texas Bowls of Red (see recipe, page 53) with this cool and icy dessert.

# Papaya Freeze

|  |  |
|---|---|
| 1 cup orange juice<br>¼ cup sugar | ● In a saucepan combine orange juice and sugar. Bring to boiling, stirring occasionally to dissolve sugar. Reduce heat and simmer for 5 minutes. Cool. |
| 1 ripe medium papaya, chopped (about 2 cups)<br>½ cup light cream<br>2 tablespoons lime juice | ● In a blender container or food processor bowl combine the chopped papaya and cream. Cover and blend or process about 1 minute or till smooth. Stir in lime juice and orange juice mixture. Transfer to a 9x9x2-inch baking pan. Cover and freeze about 2 hours or till almost firm. |
| 2 egg whites<br>¼ cup sugar | ● In a small mixer bowl beat egg whites with an electric mixer on medium speed till soft peaks form (tips curl). Gradually add sugar, beating till stiff peaks form (tips stand straight). |
| | ● Break the frozen mixture into chunks, and transfer to a chilled large mixer bowl. Beat with the electric mixer till smooth, but not melted. Fold in beaten egg whites. Return to baking pan. Cover and freeze till firm. |
| Sun Cups (optional)<br>Fried Cinnamon Chips (see recipe, page 64) (optional) | ● Let mixture stand at room temperature about 5 minutes. Serve in Sun Cups or with Fried Cinnamon Chips, if desired. Makes 6 to 8 servings. |

**Sun Cups:** Cut 6 or 8 *flour tortillas* into sun shapes with kitchen scissors (see illustration, right). In a large heavy saucepan heat 3 inches *cooking oil* to 360°. Cook tortillas, one at a time, for 30 to 45 seconds, using a ladle to hold tortillas down in the center (see photo, right). Empty ladle. Remove tortillas with tongs. Drain on paper towels.

Stir together ½ cup *sugar* and ¾ teaspoon ground *cinnamon*. Sprinkle sugar-cinnamon mixture over cups while warm. Makes 6 or 8 sun cups.

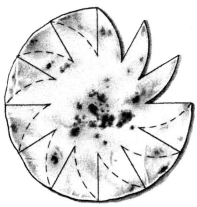

**With kitchen scissors, make about twelve 1½-inch-long cuts around tortilla (solid lines). From the *outside* tip of each cut, cut a curve (dotted lines) to the *inside* of the next cut.**

**Heat oil in a deep-fat fryer or a heavy saucepan to 360°. Fry the tortillas, one at a time, for 30 to 45 seconds or till crisp and brown. To make the cup shape, push the tortillas down in the middle with a ladle (they'll curl up around the ladle). Drain cups on paper towels.**

Sopaipillas

Pipe the dough into strips about 3 inches long and ¾ inch wide. If you like, give the pastry bag a little twist as you're piping.

Mexican Doughnut Strips

Buñuelos
*(see recipe, page 68)*

# Sopaipillas

| | |
|---|---|
| 2 cups all-purpose flour<br>1 tablespoon baking powder<br>½ teaspoon salt<br>1 tablespoon shortening<br>⅔ cup warm water<br>　(110° to 115°) | ● In a medium mixing bowl stir together flour, baking powder, and salt. Cut in shortening till thoroughly combined. Gradually add water, stirring with a fork (dough will be crumbly). |
| | ● On a lightly floured surface knead dough for 3 to 5 minutes or till smooth. Divide dough in half. Cover and let dough rest for 10 minutes.<br>　Roll each dough half into a 12½x10-inch rectangle. Using a fluted pastry wheel or knife, cut twenty 2½-inch squares from each half (do not reroll or patch dough). |
| Cooking oil for deep-fat<br>　frying<br>Sifted powdered sugar<br>Honey (optional) | ● In a heavy 3-quart saucepan fry squares, 1 or 2 at a time, in deep hot oil (425°) for 30 to 40 seconds on each side or till golden. Drain on paper towels. Sprinkle with powdered sugar. Serve warm or cool with honey, if desired. Makes 40. |

**Take it from the Test Kitchen:** The secret to making these "pillows" of bread is having the oil *very* hot and frying just a couple at a time.

# Mexican Doughnut Strips

| | |
|---|---|
| 1 cup water<br>¼ cup butter *or* margarine<br>1 tablespoon sugar<br>¼ teaspoon salt<br>1 cup all-purpose flour<br>2 eggs | ● Bring water, butter or margarine, sugar, and salt to boiling. Add flour all at once, stirring vigorously. Cook and stir with a wooden spoon till mixture forms a ball that doesn't separate. Remove from heat and cool for 10 minutes.<br>　Add the eggs, one at a time, beating well after each addition with the wooden spoon till smooth. |
| | ● Spoon dough into a pastry bag fitted with a large star tip. Pipe the dough into strips 3 inches long and ¾ inch wide onto a waxed-paper-lined baking sheet (see photo, top left). Freeze strips about 20 minutes or till they can be pulled off waxed paper. (Do not remove any strips from freezer till you're ready to fry them.) |
| Cooking oil for deep-fat<br>　frying<br>Sugar | ● In a heavy 3-quart saucepan fry dough strips, a few at a time, in deep hot oil (375°) for 3 to 4 minutes or till golden brown, turning occasionally. Drain on paper towels. Roll in sugar while warm. Makes 24. |

Street vendors sell these light and crispy pastries at festivals and markets throughout Mexico.

At *your* house, try them with a mug of steaming Mexican Hot Chocolate (see recipe, page 75).

# Buñuelos

| | | |
|---|---|---|
| **2 cups all-purpose flour**<br>**1 teaspoon baking powder**<br>**½ teaspoon salt**<br>**¼ teaspoon cream of tartar**<br>**2 tablespoons shortening**<br>**2 beaten eggs**<br>**⅓ cup milk** | ● In a mixing bowl stir together flour, baking powder, salt, and cream of tartar. Cut in shortening till thoroughly combined. Make a well in center.<br><br>In a small mixing bowl combine eggs and milk. Add to flour mixture all at once. Stir just till dough clings together. | **Don't wait till December to eat buñuelos (boon-WAY-lohs)—a favorite Mexican Christmas treat. Serve these fried sugar tortillas year-round with ice cream.** |
| | ● On a lightly floured surface knead dough about 2 minutes or till smooth. Divide dough into 24 equal portions, then shape into balls. Cover dough and let rest for 15 to 20 minutes. | |
| **Cooking oil**<br>**Cinnamon-Sugar Syrup *or***<br>**Cinnamon Sugar** | ● In a heavy 10-inch skillet heat about ¾ inch of cooking oil to 375°. Meanwhile, on a lightly floured surface roll each ball into a 4-inch circle.<br><br>Fry circles, 1 at a time, in hot oil for 1 to 1½ minutes on each side or till golden. Drain on paper towels. Drizzle with Cinnamon-Sugar Syrup or sprinkle with Cinnamon Sugar. Make and serve the same day. Makes 24. | |
| | **Cinnamon-Sugar Syrup:** In a small saucepan combine ½ cup *sugar*, ¼ cup packed *brown sugar*, ¼ cup *water*, 1 tablespoon *corn syrup*, and 3 inches *stick cinnamon* or dash ground *cinnamon*. Bring to boiling. Reduce heat and boil gently, without stirring, about 20 minutes or till thick. Discard cinnamon stick. Makes about ⅔ cup syrup. | **Be sure to serve the syrup warm, as it hardens when cooled and is difficult to reheat. Start to make the syrup while the balls of dough rest.** |
| | **Cinnamon Sugar:** In a small mixing bowl stir together ½ cup *sugar* and 1 teaspoon ground *cinnamon*. | |

# Pan Dulce

| 4 to 4½ cups all-purpose flour<br>1 package active dry yeast<br>1 cup milk<br>¼ cup sugar<br>¼ cup shortening<br>¼ teaspoon salt<br>2 eggs | ● In a large mixer bowl combine *2 cups* of flour and yeast. In a medium saucepan heat milk, sugar, shortening, and salt just till warm (115° to 120°) and shortening is almost melted, stirring constantly. Add warm milk mixture to flour mixture along with eggs.<br>　Beat with an electric mixer on low speed for ½ minute, scraping sides of bowl constantly. Beat 3 minutes at high speed. Stir in as much of the remaining flour as you can mix in with a spoon. |  |
| | ● Turn out onto a lightly floured surface. Knead in enough of the remaining flour to make a moderately stiff dough that is smooth and elastic (6 to 8 minutes total). Shape into a ball. Place in a lightly greased bowl. Turn dough once to grease surface.<br>　Cover dough and let rise in a warm place till double (1 to 1¼ hours). | **To make a seashell design in the topper of these Mexican sweet rolls, press the tip of a spoon into the topper. For a snail design, begin in the center and make a continuous spiral cut with the tip of a small knife. For a crisscross design, make parallel cuts in the topper about ½ inch apart in both directions. For a scallop design, press round scalloped cutters of various sizes into topper.** |
| **Cinnamon Topper** *or* **Orange Topper** | ● Punch dough down. Cover and let rest for 10 minutes. Divide into 16 portions. Shape each into a smooth ball. Roll or pat each ball into a 3-inch circle. Place about 2 inches apart on greased baking sheets. Use a spatula to transfer desired toppers to dough circles. Cut designs into toppers (see photo, right). Cover rolls and let rise till nearly double (30 to 40 minutes).<br>　Bake in a 375° oven for 15 to 18 minutes. Remove from sheets. Cool on wire racks. Makes 16. | |
| | **Cinnamon Topper:** Stir together ⅔ cup *all-purpose flour,* ½ cup *sugar,* and 1 tablespoon ground *cinnamon.* Cut in ¼ cup *butter or margarine* to make fine, even crumbs. Use a fork to stir in 2 beaten *egg yolks* and ½ teaspoon *vanilla.* Mix with hands till well combined. Divide mixture into 16 portions. On a lightly floured surface, roll each portion into a 3-inch circle. | |
| | **Orange Topper:** Prepare same as Cinnamon Topper, *except* substitute ½ teaspoon finely shredded *orange peel* for cinnamon and substitute 1 teaspoon *orange juice* for vanilla. | |

# Three Kings' Bread

| | | |
|---|---|---|
| 3¼ to 3¾ cups all-purpose flour<br>1 package active dry yeast<br>⅔ cup milk<br>⅓ cup butter *or* margarine<br>⅓ cup sugar<br>¼ teaspoon salt<br>2 eggs | ● In a large mixer bowl combine *1½* cups flour and yeast. In a small saucepan heat milk, butter or margarine, sugar, and salt just till warm (115° to 120°). Add to flour mixture along with eggs.<br><br>Beat with an electric mixer on low speed for ½ minute, scraping sides of bowl constantly. Beat 3 minutes on high speed. Stir in as much of the remaining flour as you can mix in with a spoon. | **January 6, the day the Three Wise Men came bearing gifts for the baby Jesus, is a gift-giving holiday in Mexico.**<br><br>**On this day, it's traditional to serve this fruit-filled Three Kings' Bread—garnished with "jewels" of candied fruit and nuts. The ring-shape bread is baked with a tiny clay or porcelain doll inside, and according to custom, whoever finds the doll must give a party on February 2.** |
| | ● Turn dough out onto a lightly floured surface. Knead in enough of the remaining flour to make a moderately soft dough that is smooth and elastic (3 to 5 minutes total). Place in a lightly greased bowl. Turn dough once to grease surface. Cover and let rise in a warm place till double (1 to 1½ hours). | **Use a piece of candy as your hidden treasure if you don't have a small doll. To place the doll or the candy in the bread, cut a small slit into the ring before frosting. Then wedge your surprise into the bread and cover the opening with icing.** |
| 2 tablespoons butter *or* margarine, melted | ● Punch dough down. Cover and let rest 10 minutes. Turn dough out onto a lightly floured surface. Roll dough into a 20x12-inch rectangle. Brush with melted butter or margarine. | |
| 2 tablespoons sugar<br>½ teaspoon ground cinnamon<br>½ cup chopped toasted almonds<br>½ cup diced mixed candied fruits and peels | ● In a small bowl combine sugar and cinnamon. Add nuts and mixed fruits and peels, tossing to coat. Sprinkle mixture over dough.<br><br>Roll the dough up jelly-roll style, beginning at a long side. Moisten edges of dough with water. Pinch together to seal firmly. Bring ends together to form a ring, and place dough, seam side down, on a greased baking sheet. Moisten and pinch ends together to seal ring well. Flatten slightly. Make cuts in dough at about 1½-inch intervals around edge (see photo, right). Cover and let rise till nearly double (30 to 40 minutes).<br><br>Bake in a 350° oven for 25 to 30 minutes, covering with foil after 15 minutes. Remove from baking sheet and cool on a wire rack. | 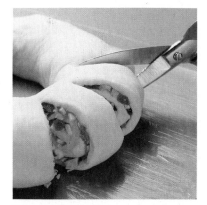<br><br>**Use scissors to snip about two-thirds of the way to the center of the ring. Make cuts every 1½ inches.** |
| 1 cup sifted powdered sugar<br>¼ teaspoon vanilla<br>Milk<br>Sliced almonds<br>Candied red *or* green cherries, halved<br>Diced candied orange peel | ● For icing, combine powdered sugar and vanilla. Stir in enough milk to make icing spreadable, then spread over ring. Before icing dries, sprinkle with almonds and decorate with candied cherries and orange peel. Makes 1 ring. | |

# Sangria

½ cup sugar
½ cup water
1 lemon, cut into ¼-inch-thick slices
1 orange, cut into ¼-inch-thick slices

● For syrup, in a small saucepan combine sugar, water, and the 4 end slices from the lemon and orange. Bring to boiling, stirring till sugar dissolves. Remove from heat and cool.
  Squeeze juice from cooked fruit slices into the syrup, then discard.

This fruity Spanish punch, bolstered with brandy, is just the thing to take the edge off Jalapeño Nachos (see recipe, page 31) or any other spicy tidbit.

1 750-milliliter bottle dry red wine, chilled
½ of a 32-ounce bottle carbonated water, chilled (2 cups)
2 tablespoons brandy
Ice cubes

● In a large pitcher or bowl combine syrup, wine, carbonated water, brandy, and remaining fruit slices. Pour over ice in wine glasses. Makes about 12 (4-ounce) servings.

# Mexican Eggnog

2 cups light cream
1 cup milk
½ cup sugar

● In a large saucepan combine cream, milk, and sugar. Heat to almost boiling, stirring occasionally. *Do not boil.*

Mexican cooks offer this drink as an after-dinner liqueur and serve it in tiny cordial glasses.

6 egg yolks

● Meanwhile, in a large mixer bowl beat egg yolks about 6 minutes or till thick and lemon colored. Gradually stir about *1 cup* of the hot cream mixture into egg yolks, then return all to saucepan. Cook and stir over low heat for 10 to 12 minutes or till mixture starts to thicken and coats a metal spoon. Cool mixture immediately by placing saucepan in a sink filled with ice water. Stir till cooled.

½ cup rum *or* brandy
½ teaspoon vanilla
  Ground cinnamon
  Ground toasted almonds *or* cashews (optional)

● Stir in rum or brandy and vanilla, then chill at least 24 hours.
  Serve in small glasses, sprinkled with cinnamon and ground nuts, if desired. Makes about 8 (4-ounce) servings.

# Tequila Sunrise *Pictured on pages 76–77.*

1⅓ cups orange juice
½ cup tequila
¼ cup lime juice
  Ice cubes
2 tablespoons grenadine
    syrup
    Carambola, sliced and
    seeds removed
    (optional)

● In a small pitcher combine orange juice, tequila, and lime juice. Pour over ice in glasses. Slowly add *1½ teaspoons* grenadine syrup to *each* glass and let it sink to the bottom.
  Garnish with carambola, if desired. Stir before drinking. Makes about 4 (4-ounce) servings.

**Pour the grenadine syrup *slowly* into each glass so it sinks to the bottom, leaving the orange juice mixture floating on top. Now *that's* a sunrise!**

# Tequila Cooler

3 cups unsweetened
    pineapple juice
2 cups unsweetened
    grapefruit juice
1 cup tequila
3 tablespoons grenadine
    syrup
  Ice cubes

● In a large pitcher combine pineapple juice, grapefruit juice, tequila, and grenadine. Pour over ice in chilled glasses. Garnish with mint sprigs, if desired. Makes about 6 (8-ounce) servings.

**Just a few sips of this Tequila Cooler and your mind will take you on a carefree vacation in sunny Acapulco—ahhhh!**

# Tequila!

Mexico and tequila—you can't have one without the other! Tequila's claim to fame is the margarita, and that cocktail's popularity is making a name for tequila outside of Mexico.

There are several types of tequila. Clear tequila, known as *white* or *silver*, comes out a powerful 104 to 106 proof after fermentation. Water is added to reduce it to 80 or 86 proof. Other varieties are aged in oak vats. The resulting pale-yellow color gives them the name *gold*. White and gold tequilas are used for cocktails. (Just for the record, this infamous liquor is distilled from the *agave* plant, *not* the cactus.)

The very best tequila is amber-colored *añejo*. It should be served straight or on the rocks.

Similar to tequila, but made in a different region of Mexico, is *mezcal*. Although this fiery concoction isn't too common outside Mexico, some brands can be purchased in the U.S. If you've ever seen a liquor bottle with a worm in the bottom, you've seen a bottle of mezcal! This agave-root worm is said to give strength to anyone brave enough to gulp it down.

# Mexican Hot Chocolate

| | |
|---|---|
| 6 cups milk<br>½ cup sugar<br>3 squares (3 ounces) unsweetened chocolate, cut up<br>1 teaspoon ground cinnamon | ● In a large saucepan combine *1 cup* milk, sugar, chocolate, and cinnamon. Cook and stir over medium-low heat till chocolate is melted. Gradually stir in remaining milk. Cook and stir till milk is very hot, almost boiling. *Do not boil.* |
| 2 beaten eggs<br>2 teaspoons vanilla | ● Gradually stir *1 cup* of the hot milk mixture into eggs, then return all to saucepan. Cook and stir for 2 minutes over low heat. Remove from heat and stir in vanilla. Beat with a *molinillo* or rotary beater till very frothy. |
| Whipped cream | ● Pour hot chocolate into mugs and dollop with whipped cream. Makes 6 (8-ounce) servings. |

To make the frothy top on this hot chocolate, Mexicans whip the mixture with a carved wooden tool called a *molinillo* (moh-lin-EE-yoh). Molinillos are still used in Mexico today, but because most American kitchens don't have one, we experimented and discovered you'll get the same effect with a rotary beater.

# Pot Coffee

| | |
|---|---|
| 6 cups water<br>¼ cup piloncillo *or* packed dark brown sugar<br>3 inches stick cinnamon<br>6 whole cloves | ● In a 3-quart saucepan combine water, piloncillo or dark brown sugar, stick cinnamon, and cloves. Heat and stir till sugar is dissolved. |
| ¾ cup ground coffee | ● Stir in coffee. Bring to boiling. Reduce heat and simmer, uncovered, 2 minutes. Remove from heat. Cover and let stand 15 minutes. Strain before serving. Makes about 5 (8-ounce) servings. |
| | **Automatic Drip Coffee:** Place ¼ cup *piloncillo or dark brown sugar,* ½ teaspoon ground *cinnamon,* and ⅛ teaspoon ground *cloves* in the coffeepot. Prepare drip coffee according to manufacturer's directions, using same amount of water and coffee as above. Let stand at least 2 minutes. |

Look for cone-shape *piloncillo* (pee-lon-SEE-yoh), unrefined Mexican sugar, in Latin American specialty stores. Chop or grate the sugar cones to get the amount you need.

**Sangrita**
*(see recipe, page 79)*

**Tequila Sunrise**
*(see recipe, page 73)*

**Mint Orangeade**
*(see recipe, page 78)*

**Frozen Margaritas**
*(see recipe, page 78)*

**Rum Punch**
*(see recipe, page 79)*

# Frozen Margaritas

*Pictured on pages 76–77.*

| | |
|---|---|
| ¾ | cup tequila |
| 1 | 6-ounce can frozen limeade concentrate |
| ½ | cup orange liqueur |

● In a blender container combine the tequila, limeade concentrate, and orange liqueur. Cover and blend till smooth.

| | |
|---|---|
| 30 | to 35 ice cubes (about 4 cups) |
| | Lime slices |

● With blender running, add the ice cubes, one at a time, through hole in lid, blending till slushy. Serve in salt-rimmed glasses* garnished with lime slices. Makes about 8 (4-ounce) servings.
*Note: To prepare glasses, rub the rim of each glass with a little *lime juice* or a *lime wedge.* Invert glasses into a shallow dish of coarse *salt.* Shake off excess salt.

**Though its Mexican origins are questioned by some nonbelievers, most of us take for granted that the margarita is the national drink of Mexico. We probably owe the creation of the libation to the custom of drinking straight tequila with salt and a wedge of lime, but a more delightful legend tells of the cocktail being invented by a man for his wife, Margarita.**

# Mint Orangeade

*Pictured on pages 76–77.*

| | |
|---|---|
| 1 | cup water |
| ⅓ | cup sugar |
| ½ | cup snipped fresh mint leaves |
| ½ | teaspoon shredded orange peel |
| 1 | cup orange juice |
| ⅓ | cup lemon juice |
| | Cracked ice |
| | Orange peel twists (optional) |
| | Mint sprigs (optional) |

● In a small saucepan combine water and sugar. Bring to boiling, stirring till sugar dissolves.
Remove from heat and pour over mint leaves. Stir in orange peel, orange juice, and lemon juice. Cover and let stand at room temperature at least 1 hour. Strain juice mixture, then cover and chill.
Serve over cracked ice. Garnish with orange peel and mint sprigs, if desired. Makes about 4 (4-ounce) servings.

**It seems like fruit is used for just about everything in Mexico—including sparkling beverages. Fruit juices, such as Mint Orangeade, are served with meals, and huge jars filled with the cool, refreshing drinks are always available in the markets, ready to quench the thirsts of the hot and tired shoppers.**

# Rum Punch

*Pictured on pages 76–77.*

1 cup boiling water
½ cup sugar

● For syrup, in a small saucepan combine water and sugar. Bring to boiling, stirring till sugar dissolves. Remove from heat and chill well.

**For a touch of the tropics, garnish each drink with a colorful miniature umbrella, or a piece of pineapple and a maraschino cherry on a cocktail pick.**

2 cups rum
1½ cups unsweetened pineapple juice
1½ cups orange juice
½ cup lemon juice *or* lime juice
1 tablespoon grenadine syrup
Ice cubes
Orange, lime, *or* lemon slices (optional)

● In a large pitcher combine syrup, rum, pineapple juice, orange juice, lemon or lime juice, and grenadine syrup. Serve over ice cubes. Garnish with orange, lime, or lemon slices, if desired. Makes about 7 (8-ounce) servings.

# Sangrita

*Pictured on pages 76–77.*

6 medium tomatoes (about 2 pounds), peeled, seeded, and coarsely cut up, *or* one 28-ounce can tomatoes
⅓ cup lime juice
1 slice of a medium onion
1 jalapeño pepper, seeded and cut up
1 teaspoon sugar
Several dashes bottled hot pepper sauce

● In a blender container place fresh tomatoes or *undrained* canned tomatoes, lime juice, onion, jalapeño pepper, sugar, and hot pepper sauce. Cover and blend till smooth.

**Chase this Mexican version of a Bloody Mary down with tequila, then suck on a lime wedge for a refresher—now that's the way they do it south of the border!**

1 cup orange juice
⅓ cup tequila
Ice cubes
Celery stalks

● Strain mixture through a sieve lined with cheesecloth. Transfer to a serving pitcher. Stir in orange juice and tequila. Serve over ice cubes with celery stalks. Makes 7 to 9 (4-ounce) servings.

# Tex-Mex Dinner

Next time you're craving the zest and spice of Tex-Mex cooking, whip up this easy-to-prepare dinner and wow friends with your cooking prowess. (See recipes on pages 82 and 83.)

**Stuffed Pork Roast**
*(see recipe, page 82)*

**Avocado-Orange Tossed Salad**
*(see recipe, page 83)*

**Tortilla Torte**
*(see recipe, page 83)*

# Tex-Mex Dinner

## MENU

Stuffed Pork Roast

Avocado-Orange Tossed
    Salad

Tortilla Torte

## MENU COUNTDOWN

*1 Week Ahead:*
Order meat for Stuffed
Pork Roast from butcher.
Ask him to loosen backbone
from rib bones.
*1 Day Ahead:*
Pick up meat at butcher's.
Prepare Tortilla Torte.
Cover and chill.
*6 Hours Ahead:*
Prepare dressing for
Avocado-Orange Tossed
Salad. Toss dressing with

orange pieces and onion
rings.
*3 Hours Ahead:*
Prepare and begin roasting
pork roast.
*15 Minutes Ahead:*
Tear salad greens. Peel,
seed, and slice avocado.
Toss avocado and greens
with dresssing mixture.
*Before Serving Dessert:*
Top torte with strawberries.

# Stuffed Pork Roast

*Pictured on pages 80–81.*

¼ cup chopped onion
¼ cup shredded carrot
1 tablespoon butter *or*
    margarine
¼ pound Homemade
    Chorizo (see recipe,
    page 8), bulk chorizo,
    *or* hot-style bulk pork
    sausage
1 cup finely chopped
    peeled apple
2 tablespoons pine nuts *or*
    slivered almonds
½ cup apple jelly
1 tablespoon chopped
    canned jalapeño pepper
1 4-pound pork loin center
    rib roast, backbone
    loosened

● For stuffing, cook onion and carrot in
butter or margarine till tender but not
brown. Remove from heat and stir in
chorizo or sausage, apple, and nuts.

For glaze, in a small saucepan stir
together jelly and jalapeño pepper. Cook
and stir over low heat till jelly is melted.

Cut 8 pockets in the meaty side of
roast between rib bones. Spoon about
*¼ cup* stuffing into *each* pocket. Place
roast, bone side down, in a shallow
roasting pan.

Insert a meat thermometer into the
roast. Roast meat, uncovered, in a 325°
oven for 2 to 2½ hours or till
thermometer registers 170°. Brush glaze
over roast several times during the last
45 minutes of roasting. Remove roast
from oven and let stand for 15 minutes.
To serve, cut meat between pockets (see
photo, right). Brush with any remaining
glaze. Makes 8 servings.

**To serve eight, get a roast
with eight rib bones so
each guest gets a full
chop. Ask your butcher to
loosen the backbone from
the rib bones. To carve,
slice the roast lengthwise
along the backbone to
separate the meat from
the bone. Slice crosswise
between pockets.**

# Avocado-Orange Tossed Salad

*Pictured on pages 80–81.*

| | | |
|---|---|---|
| 3 medium oranges | ● Finely shred peel from *1* of the oranges to make ¾ teaspoon peel. Set orange and peel aside.<br><br>Halve a *second* orange. Squeeze 1 half to get 2 tablespoons juice. Set juice aside and discard the orange shell.<br><br>Peel and slice the remaining 2½ oranges crosswise, then cut each slice into thirds. | **Hang on to any extra dressing—it's great on fruit salads or other lettuce salads.** |
| ¼ cup salad oil<br>¾ teaspoon finely shredded lemon peel<br>1 tablespoon lemon juice<br>1 tablespoon vinegar<br>2 teaspoons sugar<br>1 small red onion, sliced and separated into rings | ● For dressing, in a screw-top jar combine oil, lemon peel, lemon juice, vinegar, sugar, and reserved orange peel and orange juice. Cover and shake well.<br><br>In a medium bowl combine orange pieces and onion rings. Pour dressing over all, stirring to coat well. Cover and refrigerate for several hours, stirring occasionally. | |
| 1 medium avocado<br>5 cups torn mixed greens | ● Just before serving, drain orange and onion mixture, reserving dressing. Peel, seed, and slice avocado lengthwise.<br><br>In a large salad bowl arrange orange pieces, onion rings, and avocado slices atop the mixed greens. Drizzle with desired amount of reserved dressing. Toss to coat well. Makes 8 servings. | |

# Tortilla Torte

*Pictured on pages 80–81.*

| | | |
|---|---|---|
| 1 12-ounce package (2 cups) semisweet chocolate pieces<br>2 8-ounce cartons dairy sour cream | ● In a medium saucepan melt chocolate over low heat, stirring occasionally. Stir in sour cream. Remove from heat. Cool. | **Chill this unique dessert for several hours or overnight. The tortillas soften, which makes for easy slicing.** |
| 10 8-inch Flour Tortillas (see recipe, page 7) *or* purchased flour tortillas | ● Place 1 tortilla on a serving plate. Spread a scant ⅓ cup of the chocolate mixture atop. Repeat with remaining tortillas and chocolate mixture. | |
| ½ cup dairy sour cream<br>2 tablespoons powdered sugar<br>Fresh strawberries, halved (optional) | ● In a small mixing bowl stir together sour cream and powdered sugar. Dollop mixture atop torte. Cover and chill for several hours or overnight.<br><br>Before serving, garnish with fresh strawberries, if desired. Serves 8 to 10. | |

# Mexican Brunch

Lazy weekends are perfect for this hearty brunch since some of the food is made ahead. Stuff a tortilla with eggs and chorizo. Serve up fruit and refried beans. It all adds up to a great meal.

**Refried Beans**
*(see recipe, page 87)*

**Breakfast Burritos**
*(see recipe, page 87)*

**Fruit Compote**
*(see recipe, page 86)*

**Mock Tequila Sunrise**
*(see recipe, page 86)*

# Mexican Brunch

## MENU

Breakfast Burritos

Refried Beans

Fruit Compote

Mock Tequila Sunrise

## MENU COUNTDOWN

**5 Days Ahead:**
If desired, prepare Flour Tortillas and Homemade Chorizo for the Breakfast Burritos. Freeze tortillas and Chorizo according to directions in each recipe.
**2 Days Ahead:**
Prepare Ranchero Salsa for burritos. Cover and chill.

**1 Day Ahead:**
Prepare Fruit Compote and chill. Prepare Refried Beans.
**40 Minutes Ahead:**
Prepare burritos. Reheat beans.
**Just Before Brunch:**
Spoon compote into bowls. Prepare Mock Tequila Sunrise.

# Fruit Compote

*Pictured on pages 84–85.*

½  teaspoon finely shredded
    orange peel
2  medium oranges
3  cups peeled and sectioned
    grapefruit; peeled and
    cut-up papaya; peeled
    and sliced kiwi fruit;
    halved strawberries;
    seedless grapes; *or* fresh
    pitted dark sweet
    cherries
2  tablespoons honey
¼  teaspoon ground
    cinnamon

● Set orange peel aside. Peel and slice oranges crosswise. Place orange slices and remaining desired fruit into a plastic bag, then set the bag in a bowl.
  In a small bowl combine honey, cinnamon, and orange peel. Pour honey mixture over fruit in bag. Close bag tightly, then turn to evenly distribute honey mixture. Chill overnight, turning bag occasionally.
  To serve, spoon fruit mixture into individual bowls. Makes 6 servings.

**Prep time for this compote will vary, depending on whether you peel and section grapefruit, halve strawberries, or use whole grapes.**

# Mock Tequila Sunrise

*Pictured on pages 84–85.*

2  cups unsweetened orange
    juice
1  cup apricot nectar
3  tablespoons lemon juice
    Ice cubes
3  tablespoons grenadine
    syrup
    Lime wedges

● In a small pitcher combine orange juice, apricot nectar, and lemon juice. Pour over ice in glasses. Slowly add *1½ teaspoons* grenadine syrup to *each* glass and let it sink to the bottom. Garnish with lime wedges. Stir before drinking. Makes about 6 (4-ounce) servings.

**If your taste is more spirited, toast your brunch guests with Sangrita (see recipe, page 79) instead of this nonalcoholic orange juice drink.**

# Breakfast Burritos

*Pictured on page 84–85.*

¼ pound Homemade
  Chorizo (see recipe,
  page 8) *or* bulk chorizo
2 medium potatoes, peeled
  and finely chopped
  (about 2 cups)
½ cup chopped onion
½ cup chopped sweet red *or*
  green pepper
1 4-ounce can diced green
  chili peppers, drained
6 10-inch Flour Tortillas
  (see recipe, page 7) *or*
  purchased flour tortillas

● For filling, in a 10-inch skillet cook chorizo till it begins to brown. Stir in potatoes, onion, sweet pepper, and chili peppers. Cook, covered, over medium-low heat for 12 to 15 minutes or till potatoes are tender, stirring occasionally. Drain off fat.

  Stack tortillas and wrap tightly in foil. Heat in a 350° oven for 10 minutes to soften. (When ready to fill tortillas, remove only *half* at a time, keeping remaining ones warm in oven.)

6 beaten eggs
½ cup shredded Monterey
  Jack cheese (2 ounces)
¼ teaspoon salt
⅛ teaspoon pepper
2 tablespoons butter *or*
  margarine

● Meanwhile, in a medium mixing bowl combine eggs, cheese, salt, and pepper.

  In an 8-inch skillet melt butter or margarine over medium heat, then pour in egg mixture. Cook, without stirring, till mixture begins to set on the bottom and around edges. Lift and fold partially cooked eggs so uncooked portion flows underneath. Continue cooking over medium heat for 4 to 5 minutes or till eggs are cooked throughout but are still glossy and moist. Remove from heat.

1 medium tomato, chopped

● Spoon about *½ cup* potato mixture onto *each* tortilla just below center. Top *each* with some of the egg mixture, then sprinkle with a little tomato. Fold bottom edge of each tortilla up and over filling just till mixture is covered. Fold opposite sides of each tortilla in, just till they meet. Roll up tortillas from the bottom. Secure with wooden toothpicks.

Shredded lettuce
Ranchero Salsa (see
  recipe, page 34)
Refried Beans (optional)
  (see recipe, right)

● Arrange burritos on a baking sheet. Bake in a 350° oven for 10 to 12 minutes or till heated through.

  Remove toothpicks. Serve burritos on lettuce with Ranchero Salsa and Refried Beans, if desired. Makes 6 servings.

**Refried Beans:** In a Dutch oven combine 1 pound *dry pinto beans* and 6 cups *water*. Bring to boiling. Reduce heat and simmer for 2 minutes. Remove from heat. Cover and let stand for 1 hour. (Or, soak beans in water overnight in a covered pan.) Drain.

In same Dutch oven combine drained beans and 4 cups additional *water*. Bring to boiling. Cover and simmer for 2 hours or till very tender.

In a large heavy skillet heat ¼ cup *bacon drippings or cooking oil*. Add beans with liquid, 1½ teaspoons *salt*, and 2 cloves *garlic*, minced.

Using a potato masher, mash bean mixture completely. Cook, uncovered, for 10 to 15 minutes or till thick, stirring often. Makes 8 to 10 side-dish servings or about 5 cups.

**Mocha Almond Mousse**
*(see recipe, page 93)*

# Fire Up a Fiesta

When it comes to hosting a successful dinner party, let the old Mexican saying "Mi casa es su casa"—My house is your house—set the mood. Welcome your guests with mariachi (Mexican street band) music, brightly colored decorations, and this easy-on-the-cook-but-oh-so-delicious menu.

**Marinated Zucchini Salad**
*(see recipe, page 90)*

Avocado Soup
*(see recipe, page 91)*

Bolillos
*(see recipe, page 92)*

Fillets Stuffed with
Peppers and Cheese
*(see recipe, page 91)*

# Fire Up a Fiesta

## MENU

Avocado Soup

Fillets Stuffed with Peppers and Cheese

Marinated Zucchini Salad

Bolillos
*(see recipe, page 92)*

Mocha Almond Mousse
*(see recipe, page 93)*

## MENU COUNTDOWN

*1 Week Ahead:*
Prepare Bolillos. Wrap in heavy-duty foil and freeze.
*1 Day Ahead:*
Prepare Marinated Zucchini Salad. Cover and chill. Prepare Mocha Almond Mousse. Spoon into dessert dishes and chill.
*Morning of Party:*
Remove rolls from freezer to thaw (leave rolls in foil).
*About 3 Hours Ahead:*
Prepare Avocado Soup. Cover and chill.
*About 45 Minutes Ahead:*
Light charcoal. Assemble Fillets Stuffed with Peppers and Cheese. Cover; chill.

*15 Minutes Ahead:*
Transfer soup to a saucepan. Cook and stir till heated through. Thin soup to desired consistency by adding a little light cream or milk, if necessary.
*12 to 14 Minutes Ahead:*
Start grilling the fillets. Leaving rolls wrapped in foil, reheat in a 325° oven or, if there's room, reheat alongside fillets on grill.
*10 Minutes Ahead:*
Transfer salad to a serving platter.
*Before Serving Dessert:*
Add whipped cream and almonds to desserts.

# Marinated Zucchini Salad

*Pictured on pages 88–89.*

½ cup white wine vinegar
½ cup olive oil *or* salad oil
2 teaspoons sugar
1 teaspoon dried basil, crushed
¼ teaspoon salt
1 clove garlic, minced
2 small zucchini, halved lengthwise and sliced ¼ inch thick (2 cups)
1 cup canned garbanzo beans, drained
¼ cup sliced pitted ripe olives

● For marinade, in a screw-top jar combine vinegar, oil, sugar, basil, salt, and garlic. Cover and shake well.

In a medium mixing bowl stir together zucchini, garbanzo beans, and olives. Pour marinade over zucchini mixture, stirring to coat. Cover and refrigerate for at least 3 hours or overnight, stirring occasionally.

**For a more piquant flavor, try pimiento-stuffed olives instead of ripe olives.**

Lettuce leaves
2 tablespoons sliced green onion
2 medium tomatoes, cut into wedges

● To serve, drain zucchini mixture, reserving marinade. Spoon zucchini mixture onto a lettuce-lined platter and top with green onion and tomato wedges. Drizzle with a little of the reserved marinade. Makes 6 servings.

# Fillets Stuffed With Peppers And Cheese

*Pictured on pages 88–89.*

3 or 4 large Anaheim
    peppers, chopped, *or*
    two 4-ounce cans diced
    green chili peppers,
    drained
1 cup chopped onion
2 cloves garlic, minced
1 tablespoon cooking oil
½ cup shredded Monterey
    Jack cheese (2 ounces)
3 tablespoons fine dry bread
    crumbs
6 beef tenderloin steaks,
    cut 1 inch thick
    (about 2½ pounds)
  Salt
  Pepper

● For stuffing, in a large skillet cook peppers, onion, and garlic in oil till tender but not brown. Remove from heat and stir in cheese and bread crumbs.

Meanwhile, cut a pocket in each steak about 3 inches long and 1½ to 2 inches deep (see top photo, right). Season pockets with salt and pepper.

Put about *2 tablespoons* stuffing mixture into *each* steak pocket. Fasten pocket openings with wooden toothpicks (see bottom photo, right). Cover and chill, if desired.

● Grill steaks, on an uncovered grill, directly over *medium* coals for 5 minutes. Turn and grill to desired doneness, allowing 7 to 9 minutes more for medium. Or, broil 3 to 4 inches from heat to desired doneness, turning once (allow about 12 minutes total time for medium). Makes 6 servings.

**Use a sharp knife to cut a pocket in each fillet that's about 3 inches long and 1½ to 2 inches deep.**

**Securely close pocket openings with wooden toothpicks.**

# Avocado Soup

*Pictured on pages 88–89.*

1 14½-ounce can chicken
    broth
1 cup light cream
1 large avocado, seeded,
    peeled, and cut up
1 small onion, cut up
2 tablespoons dry sherry
  Few dashes bottled hot
    pepper sauce
  Dairy sour cream
  Snipped cilantro *or*
    parsley (optional)

● In a blender container combine the chicken broth, light cream, avocado, onion, sherry, and bottled hot pepper sauce. Cover and blend till smooth. Cover and chill, if desired.

Transfer the avocado mixture to a medium saucepan. Cook and stir over medium heat about 10 minutes or till heated through.

Dollop with sour cream and garnish with cilantro or parsley, if desired. Makes 6 side-dish servings.

**Remember this soup during the next heat wave. Serve it cold with a salad or sandwich—it makes a light, refreshing supper.**

# Bolillos

*Pictured on pages 88–89.*

7 to 7¼ cups all-purpose
   flour
2 packages active dry yeast
2½ cups water
1 tablespoon sugar
1 tablespoon shortening
½ teaspoon salt

● In a large mixer bowl combine *3 cups* of the flour and yeast. In a medium saucepan heat the water, sugar, shortening, and salt just till warm (115° to 120°) and shortening is almost melted, stirring constantly. Add to flour mixture.

    Beat with an electric mixer on low speed for ½ minute, scraping sides of bowl constantly. Beat 3 minutes at high speed. Stir in as much of the remaining flour as you can mix in with a spoon.

**On a lightly floured surface, roll each portion of dough with the palms of your hands into an oval. Pull and twist each end.**

● Turn dough out onto a lightly floured surface. Knead in enough of the remaining flour to make a stiff dough that is smooth and elastic (8 to 10 minutes total). Shape into a ball. Place in a lightly greased bowl. Turn dough once to grease surface. Cover and let rise in a warm place till double (1 to 1½ hours).

Yellow cornmeal

● Punch dough down. Cover and let rest for 10 minutes. Divide into 18 portions. Shape each into an oval about 5 inches long. Pull and twist ends slightly (see top photo, right).

    Sprinkle cornmeal over 2 greased baking sheets. Transfer rolls to baking sheets. Use a sharp knife to make a cut, ¼ inch deep, down center of each roll (see bottom photo, right).

**Slash each roll lengthwise with a sharp knife, making cuts about ¼ inch deep.**

1 egg white
1 tablespoon water

● Combine egg white and water. Brush tops and sides of rolls with egg-white-water mixture. Cover and let rise till nearly double (about 45 minutes).

    Bake in a 375° oven for 20 minutes. Brush again with egg-white-water mixture. Bake for 10 to 12 minutes more or till golden brown. Cool on wire racks. Makes 18 rolls.

# Mocha Almond Mousse

*Pictured on pages 88–89.*

¼ cup sugar
2 teaspoons instant coffee crystals
1 envelope unflavored gelatin
1¾ cups milk
4 squares (4 ounces) semisweet chocolate, cut up

● In a medium saucepan combine sugar, coffee crystals, and gelatin. Stir in milk and chocolate. Cook and stir over low heat till crystals dissolve and chocolate melts.

**No room in the fridge for all those dessert dishes? Save space by chilling the mousse in a 1½-quart soufflé dish.**

4 beaten egg yolks
¼ cup coffee liqueur
¼ teaspoon almond extract

● Gradually stir about *half* of the hot milk mixture into egg yolks, then return all to saucepan. Cook and stir for 2 to 3 minutes or till slightly thickened. *Do not boil.* Remove from heat and stir in coffee liqueur and almond extract.

Chill gelatin mixture to the consistency of corn syrup, stirring occasionally. Remove from the refrigerator (gelatin mixture will continue to set up).

4 egg whites
2 tablespoons sugar
½ cup whipping cream
Whipped cream
Sliced almonds

● Immediately beat egg whites till soft peaks form (tips curl). Gradually add sugar, beating till stiff peaks form (tips stand straight). When gelatin mixture is partially set (consistency of unbeaten egg whites), fold in stiffly beaten egg whites.

Beat ½ cup whipping cream till soft peaks form, then fold into gelatin mixture. Chill till mixture mounds slightly when spooned. Transfer to dessert dishes and chill for several hours or overnight.

To serve, dollop with whipped cream and garnish with almonds. Serves 6 to 8.

# Index

## A-B

Almond Filling, 61
Appetizers
    Cheese Crisps, 31
    Cheese Quesadillas, 32
    Chorizo and Cheese
      Quesadillas, 32
    Guacamole, 18
    Jalapeño Nachos, 31
    Marinated Seafood, 32
    Meaty Nachos, 31
Automatic Drip Coffee, 75
Avocado-Orange Tossed
    Salad, 83
Avocado Soup, 91
Baked Chiles Rellenos, 57
Beans, Refried, 87
Beef
    Beef Chimichangas, 13
    Beef Stew in a Pot, 43
    Fillets Stuffed with Peppers
      and Cheese, 91
    Meatball Soup, 42
    Meaty Nachos, 31
    New Mexican Enchiladas, 20
    Northerners' Chili, 53
    Picadillo, 14
    Picadillo Chimichangas, 14
    Sizzling Beef Fajitas, 18
    Stuffed Peppers with Walnut
      Topper, 52
    Super Burritos, 12
    Texas Bowls of Red, 53
Beverages
    Automatic Drip Coffee, 75
    Frozen Margaritas, 78
    Mexican Eggnog, 72
    Mexican Hot Chocolate, 75
    Mint Orangeade, 78

Beverages (continued)
    Mock Tequila Sunrise, 86
    Pot Coffee, 75
    Rum Punch, 79
    Sangria, 72
    Sangrita, 79
    Tequila Cooler, 73
    Tequila Sunrise, 73
Bolillos, 92
Breads
    Bolillos, 92
    Buñuelos, 68
    Corn Tortillas, 6
    Flour Tortillas, 7
    Mexican Doughnut Strips, 67
    Pan Dulce, 69
    Sopaipillas, 67
    Three Kings' Bread, 71
Breakfast Burritos, 87
Buñuelos, 68
Burritos
    Breakfast Burritos, 87
    Burrito Sauce, 12
    Super Burritos, 12

## C

Cheese Crisps, 31
Cheese Quesadillas, 32
Chicken
    Chicken Baked in Banana
      Leaves, 46
    Chicken Enchiladas with Green
      Sauce, 22
    Chicken Flautas, 10
    Chicken Tostadas, 15
    Chicken with Mole Sauce, 48
    Chicken with Pumpkin Seed
      Sauce, 49
    Lime Soup, 40
    Marinated Chicken Tacos, 9
    Mexican Chicken Soup, 39
    Savory Chicken Tamales, 26
    Spicy-Hot Chicken Fajitas, 19
    Tablecloth-Stainer Stew, 45

Chili, Northerners', 53
Chimichangas, Beef, 13
Chimichangas, Picadillo, 14
Chocolate-Cinnamon Ice Cream, 64
Chorizo
    Breakfast Burritos, 87
    Chorizo and Cheese
      Quesadillas, 32
    Chorizo Tacos, 8
    Homemade Chorizo, 8
Cinnamon
    Chocolate-Cinnamon Ice
      Cream, 64
    Cinnamon-Apricot Filling, 61
    Cinnamon Sugar, 68
    Cinnamon-Sugar Syrup, 68
    Cinnamon Topper, 69
Classic Tamales, 24
Corn Soup, 38
Corn Tortillas, 6
Creamy Seafood Enchiladas, 23

## D-G

Desserts
    Buñuelos, 68
    Chocolate-Cinnamon Ice
      Cream, 64
    Dessert Empanadas, 61
    Flaming Plantains, 60
    Flan, 59
    Fried Cinnamon Chips, 64
    Fried Ice Cream, 62
    Mexican Doughnut Strips, 67
    Mexican Wedding Cookies, 60
    Mocha Almond Mousse, 93
    Pan Dulce, 69
    Papaya Freeze, 65
    Sopaipillas, 67
    Sun Cups, 65
    Sweet Tamales with Lemon
      Sauce, 27

Desserts *(continued)*
    Tequila Sunrise Slush, 64
    Three Kings' Bread, 71
    Tortilla Torte, 83
Drunken Fish, 55
Eggnog, Mexican 72
Empanadas, Dessert, 61
Enchiladas
    Chicken Enchiladas with Green
      Sauce, 22
    Creamy Seafood Enchiladas, 23
    New Mexican Enchiladas, 20
Fajitas, Sizzling Beef, 18
Fajitas, Spicy-Hot Chicken, 19
Fillets Stuffed with Peppers
    and Cheese, 91
Fish and Seafood
    Creamy Seafood Enchiladas, 23
    Drunken Fish, 55
    Marinated Seafood, 32
    Snapper Veracruz, 56
Flaming Plantains, 60
Flan, 59
Flour Tortillas, 7
Fried Cinnamon Chips, 64
Fried Ice Cream, 62
Frozen Margaritas, 78
Fruit Compote, 86
Garlic Soup, 42
Green Chili Sauce, 35
Green Sauce, 22
Guacamole, 18

# H-R

Homemade Chorizo, 8
Homemade Salsa, 36
Hot Chocolate, Mexican, 75
Huevos Rancheros, 57

Ice Cream, Chocolate-Cinnamon, 64
Jalapeño Nachos, 31
Lemon Sauce, 27
Lime Soup, 40
Main Dishes
    Baked Chiles Rellenos, 57
    Beef Chimichangas, 13
    Beef Stew in a Pot, 43
    Breakfast Burritos, 87
    Chicken Baked in Banana
      Leaves, 46
    Chicken Enchiladas with Green
      Sauce, 22
    Chicken Flautas, 10
    Chicken Tostadas, 15
    Chicken with Mole Sauce, 48
    Chicken with Pumpkin Seed
      Sauce, 49
    Chorizo Tacos, 8
    Creamy Seafood Enchiladas, 23
    Drunken Fish, 55
    Fillets Stuffed with Peppers
      and Cheese, 91
    Huevos Rancheros, 57
    Lime Soup, 40
    Marinated Chicken Tacos, 9
    Meatball Soup, 42
    Mexican Chicken Soup, 39
    New Mexican Enchiladas, 20
    Northerners' Chili, 53
    One-Pot Spanish Ribs, 50
    Picadillo Chimichangas, 14
    Pork and Hominy Soup, 38
    Pork and Peppers, 49
    Pork Chops in Adobo Sauce, 51
    Savory Chicken Tamales, 26
    Sizzling Beef Fajitas, 18
    Snapper Veracruz, 56
    Spicy-Hot Chicken Fajitas, 19
    Stuffed Peppers with Walnut
      Topper, 52

Main Dishes *(continued)*
    Stuffed Pork Roast, 82
    Super Burritos, 12
    Tablecloth-Stainer Stew, 45
    Texas Bowls of Red, 53
Margaritas, Frozen, 78
Marinated Chicken Tacos, 9
Marinated Seafood, 32
Marinated Zucchini Salad, 90
Meatball Soup, 42
Meaty Nachos, 31
Menus
    Fire Up a Fiesta, 88
    Mexican Brunch, 84
    Tex-Mex Dinner, 80
Mexican Chicken Soup, 39
Mexican Doughnut Strips, 67
Mexican Eggnog, 72
Mexican Hot Chocolate, 75
Mexican Wedding Cookies, 60
Mint Orangeade, 78
Mocha Almond Mousse, 93
Mock Tequila Sunrise, 86
Mole Sauce, 48
Nachos, Jalapeño, 31
Nachos, Meaty, 31
New Mexican Enchiladas, 20
Northerners' Chili, 53
One-Pot Spanish Ribs, 50
Orange Topper, 69
Pan Dulce, 69
Papaya Freeze, 65
Picadillo, 14
Picadillo Chimichangas, 14
Picante Sauce, 34
Pico de Gallo Salsa, 35

Pork
  Breakfast Burritos, 87
  Chorizo and Cheese
    Quesadillas, 32
  Chorizo Tacos, 8
  Homemade Chorizo, 8
  One-Pot Spanish Ribs, 50
  Pork and Hominy Soup, 38
  Pork and Peppers, 49
  Pork Chops in Adobo Sauce, 51
  Stuffed Pork Roast, 82
  Tablecloth-Stainer Stew, 45
Pot Coffee, 75
Pumpkin Filling, 61
Pumpkin Seed Sauce, 49
Quesadillas, Cheese, 32
Quesadillas, Chorizo and Cheese, 32
Ranchero Salsa, 34
Red Chili Sauce, 35
Refried Beans, 87
Rum Punch, 79

**S**

Salad, Avocado-Orange Tossed, 83
Salad, Marinated Zucchini, 90
Salsas
  Homemade Salsa, 36
  Pico de Gallo Salsa, 35
  Ranchero Salsa, 34
  Salsa Verde, 36
Sangria, 72
Sangrita, 79
Sauces
  Adobo Sauce, 51
  Burrito Sauce, 12
  Green Chili Sauce, 35
  Green Sauce, 22
  Lemon Sauce, 27
  Mole Sauce, 48

Sauces (continued)
  Picante Sauce, 34
  Pumpkin Seed Sauce, 49
  Red Chili Sauce, 35
  Walnut Topper, 52
Savory Chicken Tamales, 26
Seafood, Marinated, 32
Side Dishes
  Avocado Soup, 91
  Avocado-Orange Tossed
    Salad, 83
  Corn Soup, 38
  Fruit Compote, 86
  Garlic Soup, 42
  Marinated Zucchini Salad, 90
  Refried Beans, 87
  Tortilla Soup, 41
Sizzling Beef Fajitas, 18
Snapper Veracruz, 56
Sopaipillas, 67
Soups and Stews
  Avocado Soup, 91
  Beef Stew in a Pot, 43
  Corn Soup, 38
  Garlic Soup, 42
  Lime Soup, 40
  Meatball Soup, 42
  Mexican Chicken Soup, 39
  Northerners' Chili, 53
  Pork and Hominy Soup, 38
  Tablecloth-Stainer Stew, 45
  Texas Bowls of Red, 53
  Tortilla Soup, 41
Spicy-Hot Chicken Fajitas, 19
Stuffed Peppers with Walnut
  Topper, 52
Stuffed Pork Roast, 82
Sun Cups, 65
Super Burritos, 12
Sweet Tamales with Lemon
  Sauce, 27

**T-Z**

Tablecloth-Stainer Stew, 45
Tacos, Chorizo, 8
Tacos, Marinated Chicken, 9
Tamales
  Classic Tamales, 24
  Savory Chicken Tamales, 26
  Sweet Tamales with Lemon
    Sauce, 27
Tequila
  Frozen Margaritas, 78
  Sangrita, 79
  Tequila Cooler, 73
  Tequila Sunrise, 73
  Tequila Sunrise Slush, 64
Texas Bowls of Red, 53
Three Kings' Bread, 71
Tortillas
  Corn Tortillas, 6
  Flour Tortillas, 7
  Tortilla Soup, 41
  Tortilla Torte, 83
Tostadas, Chicken, 15
Walnut Topper, 52

**Tips**

Chili Pepper Identification, 29
It's All in the Roll, 4
Let's Have a Taco Fiesta!, 9
Make Mine Vanilla, 58
Tequila!, 73
Top It Off, 11
Working with Chili Peppers, 30